IB Mathematics HL

in **130** pages

2018-2020

No part of this publication may be reproduced, stored in a retrieval system, or transmitted, in any form or by any means, electronic, mechanical, photocopying, recording, or otherwise, without the prior written permission of the author.

This book has been developed independently of the International Baccalaureate® Organization (IBO), and the content is in no way connected with nor endorsed by the International Baccalaureate® Organization (IBO).

While every attempt has been made to trace and acknowledge copyright, the author apologizes for any accidental infringement where the copyright has proved untraceable.

Cover Image: iStock.com/Tramont_ana

1ˢᵗ Ed.(July 2019)

CONTENTS

Introduction

This revision guide will be a valuable resource and reference for students, assisting them in understanding and learning the theory of IB mathematics HL.

The ideal preparation for any student preparing for the IB math exams is to systematically practice doing questions from past papers. Similar exercises can be found in any IB mathematics HL textbook and on official distributor sites for IB materials.

The guide aims to help the IB student by both revising the theory and going through some well-chosen examples of the IB mathematics HL curriculum.

I have made a concerted effort to explain the mathematical terms to the student in a **clear, straightforward, and understandable manner**. My aim is to create a **thorough** and **concise** material with an emphasis on simplicity, which will be effective for both teachers and students.

By presenting the theory that every IB student should know before taking any quiz, test, or exam, this revision guide is designed to make the topics of IB mathematics HL both comprehensible and easy to grasp.

George Feretzakis, July 2019

"Truth is ever to be found in the simplicity, and not in the multiplicity and confusion of things."

Isaac Newton

The best IB Math revision guide app, with video lessons, many calculators, solvers, and it is **100% free**, **No** in-app purchases, **No** advertisements.

Useful Formulas & Rounding

$(a \pm b)^2 = a^2 \pm 2ab + b^2$	$a^2 - b^2 = (a + b)(a - b)$
$(a + b + c)^2 = a^2 + b^2 + c^2 + 2ab + 2ac + 2bc$	$a^3 - b^3 = (a - b)(a^2 + ab + b^2)$

Area of a parallelogram		Volume of a cylinder	
	$A = b \times h$		$V = \pi r^2 h$
Area of a triangle		Volume of a cuboid	
	$A = \dfrac{1}{2}(b \times h)$		$V = l \times w \times h$
Area of a trapezium		Area of the curved surface of a cylinder	
	$A = \dfrac{1}{2}(a + b) \times h$		$A = 2\pi rh$
Area of a circle		Volume of a sphere	
	$A = \pi r^2$		$V = \dfrac{4}{3}\pi r^3$
Circumference of a circle		Volume of a cone	
	$C = 2\pi r$		$V = \dfrac{1}{3}\pi r^2 h$

Surface area of a sphere	$A = 4\pi r^2$	Area of the curved surface of a cone	$A = \pi r l$
Volume of a pyramid	$V = \dfrac{1}{3}(Area) \times h$	Volume of a prism	$V = (Area) \times h$

Significant Figure Rules *

There are three rules for determining how many significant figures are in a number:

1. Non-zero digits are always significant.

2. Any zeros between two significant digits are significant.

3. A final zero or trailing zeros in the decimal portion only are significant.

Trailing zeros are a sequence of 0s in the decimal representation of a number, after which no other digits follow.

Example 1	Example 2
1254.04 rounded to 5 s.f. is 1254.0	0.030503062 rounded to 5 s.f. is 0.030503
1254.04 rounded to 4 s.f. is 1254	0.030503062 rounded to 4 s.f. is 0.03050
1254.04 rounded to 3 s.f. is 1250	0.030503062 rounded to 3 s.f. is 0.0305
1254.04 rounded to 2 s.f. is 1300	0.030503062 rounded to 2 s.f. is 0.031
1254.04 rounded to 1 s.f. is 1000	0.030503062 rounded to 1 s.f. is 0.03

* You can download our **app** using the QR code on page 1, where there is a calculator that can round any number to as many significant figures as desired using proper rounding rules. Apart from the aforementioned calculator, our app has many other **solvers** and **calculators** accompanied by the corresponding theory.

Straight Lines

The equation of a straight line is usually written:

$$y = mx + c$$

where m is the **slope** or gradient and c is the **y-intercept**.

Another way to find the equation of a straight line is the following:

$$y - y_0 = m(x - x_0)$$

where m is the slope and (x_0, y_0) is a point which lies on the line.

To find the **slope m**, you use the following formula:

$$m = \frac{y_2 - y_1}{x_2 - x_1} = \frac{rise}{run}$$

where (x_1, y_1) and (x_2, y_2) are two points which lie on the line.

Note: When a line has a **positive** slope, it rises left to right (its graph will be **increasing**).

When a line has a **negative** slope, it falls left to right (its graph will be **decreasing**).

The **slope** (or gradient) m describes both the direction and the steepness of the line and is related to its angle of incline θ by the tangent function.

$$m = \tan(\theta)$$

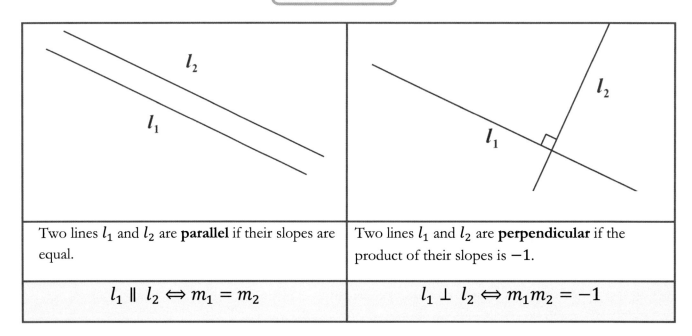

Two lines l_1 and l_2 are **parallel** if their slopes are equal.	Two lines l_1 and l_2 are **perpendicular** if the product of their slopes is -1.
$l_1 \parallel l_2 \Leftrightarrow m_1 = m_2$	$l_1 \perp l_2 \Leftrightarrow m_1 m_2 = -1$

A **horizontal** line graph has an equation of the following form, and its **slope is zero**.	A **vertical** line graph has an equation of the following form, and it has an **undefined slope** (no slope).
$y = c$	$x = c$

Midpoint Formula: The coordinates of the **midpoint M** of two points $A(x_1, y_1, z_1)$ and $B(x_2, y_2, z_2)$, are given by the following formula:

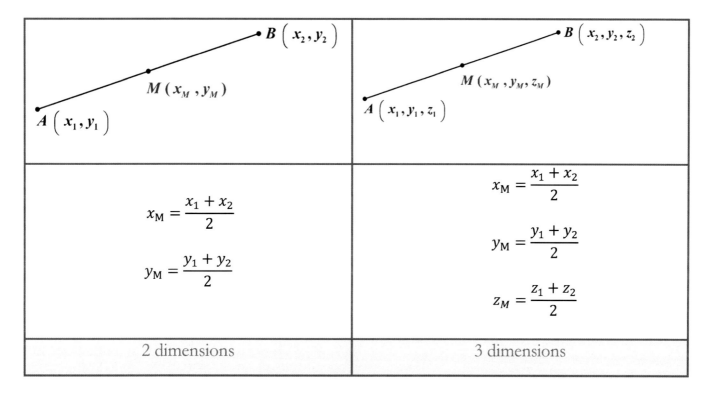

$x_M = \dfrac{x_1 + x_2}{2}$ $y_M = \dfrac{y_1 + y_2}{2}$	$x_M = \dfrac{x_1 + x_2}{2}$ $y_M = \dfrac{y_1 + y_2}{2}$ $z_M = \dfrac{z_1 + z_2}{2}$
2 dimensions	3 dimensions

Distance Formula: Given two points $A(x_1, y_1, z_1)$ and $B(x_2, y_2, z_2)$, the distance (d) between these two points is given by the formula:

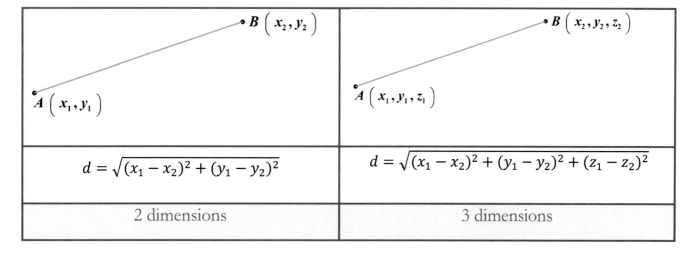

$d = \sqrt{(x_1 - x_2)^2 + (y_1 - y_2)^2}$	$d = \sqrt{(x_1 - x_2)^2 + (y_1 - y_2)^2 + (z_1 - z_2)^2}$
2 dimensions	3 dimensions

Quadratic Functions

A quadratic function is of the form

$$f(x) = ax^2 + bx + c, \text{ where } a, b, c \in \mathbb{R} \text{ and } a \neq 0.$$

The graph of a quadratic function is a curve called a parabola. Parabolas may open upward or downward, and all have the same basic "**U**" shape.

If **a** is **positive**, the graph **opens upward** (Figure 1), and if **a** is **negative** (Figure 2), then it **opens downward**.

The **y-intercept** of the above function is **c**.

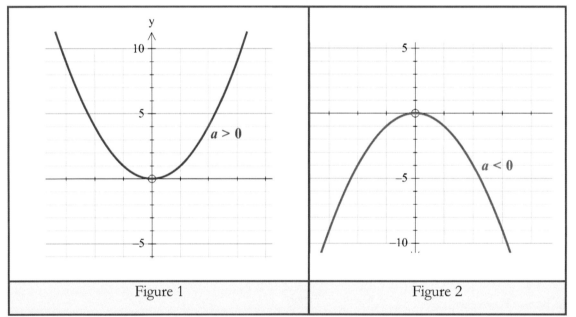

Figure 1	Figure 2

All parabolas are symmetric with respect to a line called the **axis of symmetry**, with the equation:

$$x = \frac{-b}{2a}$$

A parabola intersects its axis of symmetry at a point called the vertex **V** of the parabola, which has coordinates:

$$V\left(\frac{-b}{2a}, f\left(\frac{-b}{2a}\right)\right)$$

The three most common forms that are used to express quadratic functions are:

Standard form: $f(x) = ax^2 + bx + c$

Factored form: $f(x) = a(x - r_1)(x - r_2)$, where r_1, r_2 are the two distinct real roots which are the x-intercepts of the graph $f(x)$. The equation of the axis of symmetry (i.e., the x-coordinate of the vertex) passes through the mid-point of the roots of the parabola.

$f(x) = a(x - r)^2$, where r is a real double root (two equal real roots) which is the x-intercept of the graph of $f(x)$.

Vertex form: $f(x) = a(x - h)^2 + k$, where h, k are the coordinates of the vertex $V(h, k)$.

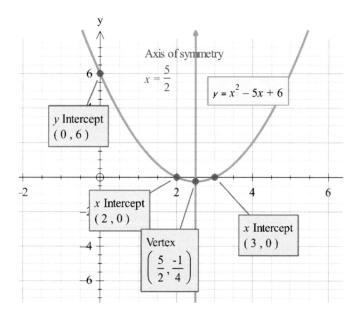

For example, the quadratic function $f(x) = x^2 - 5x + 6$ can be written as:

Standard form: $f(x) = x^2 - 5x + 6$

Factored form: $f(x) = 1(x - 2)(x - 3)$, where $2, 3$ are the two roots.

Vertex form: $f(x) = 1(x - \frac{5}{2})^2 - \frac{1}{4}$, where the vertex V has coordinates $(\frac{5}{2}, -\frac{1}{4})$.

Note: We observe that the x-coordinate of the vertex is the midpoint of the two roots, $\frac{2+3}{2} = \frac{5}{2}$.

Quadratic Equations & Inequalities

To **solve a quadratic equation** of the form $ax^2 + bx + c = 0$ follow these steps:

1. When the **discriminant** $(\Delta = b^2 - 4ac)$ is **positive** $(\Delta > 0)$ then the equation has two distinct real roots r_1 and r_2.

$$r_{1,2} = \frac{-b \pm \sqrt{b^2 - 4ac}}{2a}$$

2. When the **discriminant** is equal to **zero** $(\Delta = 0)$ then the equation has one double (two equal real roots) root r.

$$r = \frac{-b}{2a}$$

3. When the **discriminant** is **negative** $(\Delta < 0)$ then the equation has no real roots.

To **solve a quadratic inequality** of the form $ax^2 + bx + c \geq 0$ or $ax^2 + bx + c \leq 0$ follow these steps:

I. When the discriminant is positive $(\Delta > 0)$ then the corresponding quadratic equation $(ax^2 + bx + c = 0)$ has two distinct real roots r_1 and r_2.

In this case the quadratic function $f(x) = ax^2 + bx + c$ has the opposite sign of $\boldsymbol{a}$ between the two real roots and the same sign as $\boldsymbol{a}$ outside the interval (r_1, r_2).

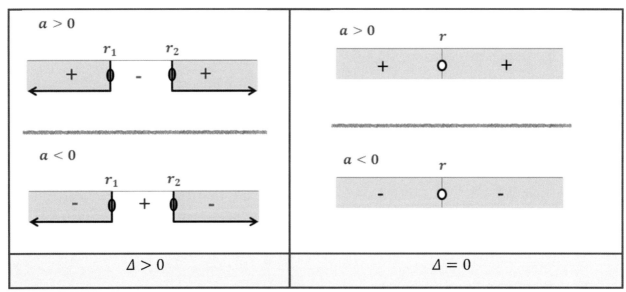

II.   When the discriminant is equal to zero $(\varDelta = 0)$ then the corresponding quadratic equation has one double (two equal real roots) real root r. In this case the, quadratic function f has the same sign as $\boldsymbol{a}$ for any value of x except $-\frac{b}{2a}$ since $f\left(-\frac{b}{2a}\right) = 0$.

III.   When the discriminant is negative $(\varDelta < 0)$ then the corresponding quadratic equation has no real roots. In this case, the quadratic function f has the same sign as $\boldsymbol{a}$ regardless of the values of x.

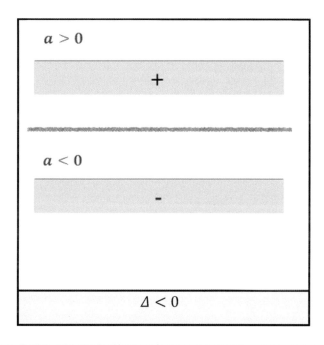

The intersection of a Line and a Parabola

The intersection between a **line** with equation $y = mx + d$ and a **parabola** with equation $y = ax^2 + bx + c$ is obtained by setting them equal to each other.

$$ax^2 + bx + c = mx + d \Rightarrow ax^2 + (b - m)x + (c - d) = 0$$

The line intersects the parabola at two points maximum.

▪   If the discriminant of the quadratic equation above is negative $(\varDelta < 0)$, then the parabola does not meet the line.

▪   If the discriminant of the quadratic equation above is positive $(\varDelta > 0)$, then the line intersects the parabola in two distinct points.

▪   If the discriminant of the quadratic equation above is zero $(\varDelta = 0)$, then the line is tangent to the parabola (touches the parabola at only one point).

Vieta's Formulas {François Viète (1540 –1603)}

Vieta's Formulas can be used to relate the sum and product of the roots of a polynomial to its coefficients.

Let α, β be the roots of the following **quadratic** equation

$$ax^2 + bx + c = 0$$

Then the Sum and the Product of the roots can be expressed as:

$$S = \alpha + \beta = -\frac{b}{a} \qquad P = \alpha\beta = \frac{c}{a}$$

The quadratic equation with roots α, β can be written as:

$$x^2 - Sx + P = 0$$

Let α, β, γ be the roots of the following **cubic** equation

$$ax^3 + bx^2 + cx + d = 0$$

Then the Sums (S_1), (S_2) and the Product (P) of the roots can be expressed as:

$$S_1 = \alpha + \beta + \gamma = -\frac{b}{a} \qquad S_2 = \alpha\beta + \beta\gamma + \gamma\alpha = \frac{c}{a} \qquad P = \alpha\beta\gamma = -\frac{d}{a}$$

The cubic equation with roots α, β, γ can be written as:

$$x^3 - S_1 x^2 + S_2 x - P = 0$$

Let $r_1, r_2, .., r_n$ be the roots of the following n^{th} **degree polynomial** equation

$$P(x) = a_n x^n + a_{n-1} x^{n-1} + \cdots + a_1 x + a_0 = 0$$

Then the Sum (S) and the Product (P) of the roots can be expressed as:

$$S = r_1 + r_2 + .. + r_n = -\frac{a_{n-1}}{a_n} \qquad P = r_1 r_2 \cdots r_n = (-1)^n \frac{a_0}{a_n}$$

Polynomials

A **polynomial** in the variable x, denoted by $p(x)$, is expressed as follows:

Leading coefficient   Degree

$$p(x) = a_n x^n + a_{n-1} x^{n-1} + \ldots + a_2 x^2 + a_1 x + a_0$$

Leading term

- The powers of x are positive integers.
- The real numbers $a_n, a_{n-1}, \ldots, a_2, a_1, a_0$ appearing in each term in front of the variable are called the **coefficients**.
- The greatest power of the variable is the **degree** of the polynomial.

For any **polynomial division** holds:

$$D(x) = d(x) \times q(x) + r(x)$$

$$\frac{D(x)}{d(x)} = q(x) + \frac{r(x)}{d(x)}$$

where

$D(x): Dividend,\ d(x): divisor,\ q(x): quotient$ and $r(x): remainder$

Note: The degree of the Dividend $D(x)$ is greater than or equal to the degree of the divisor $d(x)$ and the degree of the remainder $r(x)$ is less than the degree of the divisor $d(x)$.

The Factor Theorem

Suppose $p(x)$ is a nonzero polynomial.

The real number α is a zero of $p(x)$ if and only if $(x - \alpha)$ is a factor of $p(x)$.

Example

If the polynomial $p(x) = 2x^3 + kx^2 + 5x - 6$ has a factor $x + 2$, find the value of k.

Solution

Since $x + 2$ is a factor of $p(x)$ then $p(-2) = 0$

$$p(-2) = 2(-2)^3 + k(-2)^2 + 5(-2) - 6 = 0$$

$$-16 + 4k - 10 - 6 = 0 \Rightarrow 4k = 32 \Rightarrow k = 8$$

The Remainder Theorem

Suppose $p(x)$ is a polynomial of degree at least 1 and a real number α. When $p(x)$ is divided by $(x - \alpha)$ the remainder is $p(\alpha)$.

Example

Find the remainder when $x^{30} + 3x^5 + 6$ is divided by $x + 1$.

Solution

If $p(x) = x^{30} + 3x^5 + 6$, then $p(-1) = (-1)^{30} + 3(-1)^5 + 6 = 1 - 3 + 6 = 4$

Rational-Root Theorem (Optional)

Let a polynomial $p(x) = a_n x^n + a_{n-1} x^{n-1} + \cdots + a_1 x + a_0$

Where $a_0, a_1, \dots, a_n$ are integers with $a_n \neq 0$ and $a_0 \neq 0$.

If $\frac{k}{m}$ is a root of $p(x) = 0$ in lowest terms, then k is a factor of constant term a_0 and m is a factor of leading coefficient a_n.

Note: The **Rational-Root Theorem** gives a way to yield the possible rational roots of a polynomial. It does not determine which of these possible roots are actual roots of the polynomial and it says nothing about roots that are not rational.

Example: List all possible rational zeros of the following polynomial

$$4x^3 - 9x^2 + 6x - 1 = 0$$

Solution: Factors of the constant term: ± 1, factors of the leading coefficient: $\pm 1, \pm 2, \pm 4$

The possible rational roots are (values of $\frac{k}{m}$): $\pm \frac{1}{1}, \pm \frac{1}{2}, \pm \frac{1}{4}$

The actual roots (zeros) of the above polynomial equation are: 1 (double root) and $\frac{1}{4}$.

Long division of Polynomials

$x + 1 \overline{\smash{)}2x^3 + 9x^2 - 15}$	First, we arrange each term of the dividend from highest to lowest degree.
$x + 1 \overline{\smash{)}2x^3 + 9x^2 + 0x - 15}$	The missed terms are written with zero coefficients.
$\begin{array}{r} 2x^2 \\ x + 1 \overline{\smash{)}2x^3 + 9x^2 + 0x - 15} \\ (-)\, 2x^3 + 2x^2 \\ \hline 7x^2 + 0x - 15 \end{array}$	To begin the division, divide the leading term of the dividend by the leading term of the divisor: $\dfrac{2x^3}{x} = 2x^2$. The first term of the quotient $(2x^2)$ goes above the division bracket and is aligned with the corresponding dividend term $(2x^3)$. We then multiply this term $(2x^2)$ by the entire divisor $(x+1)$ and write the result $(2x^3 + 2x^2)$ under the corresponding terms of the dividend. Then we subtract the dividend from the obtained result.
$\begin{array}{r} 2x^2 + 7x \\ x + 1 \overline{\smash{)}2x^3 + 9x^2 + 0x - 15} \\ (-)\, 2x^3 + 2x^2 \\ \hline 7x^2 + 0x - 15 \\ (-)\, 7x^2 + 7x \\ \hline \text{-}7x - 15 \end{array}$	The previous step is repeated until the remainder is of a lesser degree than the divisor. Divide the leading term of the dividend by the leading term of the divisor: $\dfrac{7x^2}{x} = 7x$. We then multiply this term $(7x)$ by the entire divisor $(x+1)$ and write the result $(7x^2 + 7x)$ under the corresponding terms of the last result. Then we subtract the remainder from the obtained result.
$\begin{array}{r} 2x^2 + 7x - 7 \\ x + 1 \overline{\smash{)}2x^3 + 9x^2 + 0x - 15} \\ (-)\, 2x^3 + 2x^2 \\ \hline 7x^2 + 0x - 15 \\ (-)\, 7x^2 + 7x \\ \hline \text{-}7x - 15 \\ (-)\, -7x - 7 \\ \hline \text{-}8 \end{array}$	The previous step is repeated for the last time. Divide the leading term of the dividend by the leading term of the divisor: $\dfrac{-7x}{x} = -7$. We then multiply this term (7) by the entire divisor $(x+1)$ and write the result $(-7x - 7)$ under the corresponding terms of the last result. Then we subtract the remainder from the obtained result. Our quotient is $2x^2 + 7x - 7$, and the remainder is -8.
$\underbrace{\dfrac{2x^3 + 9x^2 - 15}{\underset{\text{divisor}}{x + 1}}}_{\text{Dividend}} = \underbrace{2x^2 + 7x - 7}_{\text{quotient}} + \underbrace{\dfrac{\text{-}8}{\underset{\text{divisor}}{x + 1}}}_{\text{remainder}}$	$\underbrace{(2x^3 + 9x^2 - 15)}_{\text{Dividend}} = \underbrace{(2x^2 + 7x - 7)}_{\text{quotient}}\underbrace{(x + 1)}_{\text{divisor}} + \underbrace{(\text{-8})}_{\text{remainder}}$

Synthetic division

To find the quotient and remainder when a polynomial is divided by $x - a$, a shortened version of the long division called synthetic division makes the task easier. The only drawback to synthetic division is that it works only for linear binomials as divisors. We'll do the same division as before, but using synthetic division this time.

$-1 \mid$ 2 9 0 -15	First, we copy the coefficients from the terms in descending order. Use zeros for missing terms. Find the root associated with the divisor. i.e., $x + 1 = 0 \Rightarrow x = -1$.
$-1 \mid$ 2 9 0 -15 2	We bring down the first number, **2**.

$-1 \mid$ 2 9 0 -15
    -2
  2 7
	Multiply this number (2) by (-1) , write the product below the second coefficient and add these numbers
	
	$(9 + (-2) = 7)$.

$-1 \mid$ 2 9 0 -15
    -2 -7
  2 7 -7
	We repeat this process, multiplying each sum by (-1) and adding, until we run out of coefficients.

$-1 \mid$ 2 9 0 -15
    -2 -7 7
  2 7 -7 $\boxed{-8}$
	The bottom row represents the coefficients of the quotient, and the last number (-8) of the bottom row is the remainder. The quotient starts with leading term one degree less than the dividend. In this example, the quotient is $2x^2 + 7x - 7$, and the remainder is -8.
	
	This is the same answer we got doing long division.

$\dfrac{\overset{\text{Dividend}}{2x^3 + 9x^2 - 15}}{\underset{\text{divisor}}{x + 1}} = \overset{\text{quotient}}{2x^2 + 7x - 7} + \dfrac{\overset{\text{remainder}}{-8}}{\underset{\text{divisor}}{x + 1}}$	$\overset{\text{Dividend}}{(2x^3 + 9x^2 - 15)} = \overset{\text{quotient}}{(2x^2 + 7x - 7)}\overset{\text{divisor}}{(x + 1)} + \overset{\text{remainder}}{(-8)}$

End Behavior of Polynomials

The **end behavior** of a nth-degree polynomial function $p(x)$ with leading coefficient a_n is determined by the sign of the leading coefficient and its degree.

$$p(x) = a_n x^n + a_{n-1} x^{n-1} + \cdots + a_1 x + a_0 = 0$$

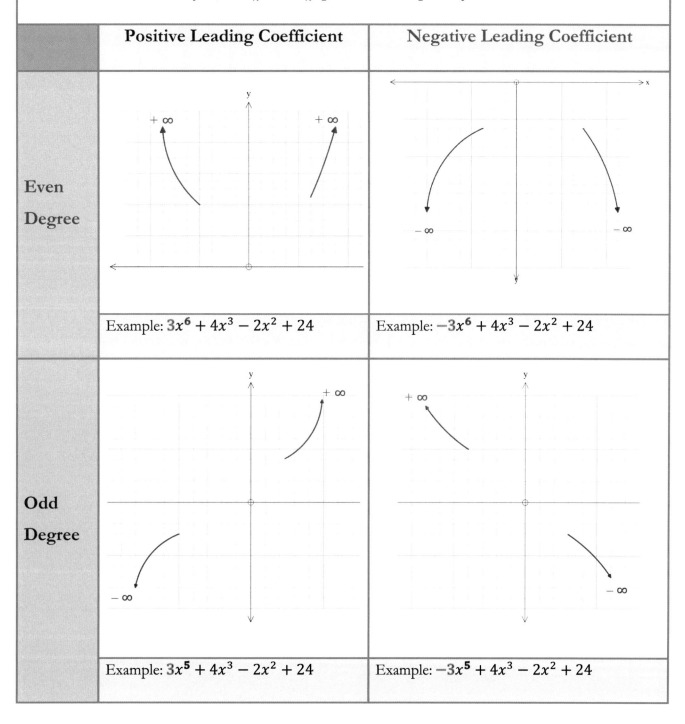

	Positive Leading Coefficient	**Negative Leading Coefficient**
Even Degree	Example: $3x^6 + 4x^3 - 2x^2 + 24$	Example: $-3x^6 + 4x^3 - 2x^2 + 24$
Odd Degree	Example: $3x^5 + 4x^3 - 2x^2 + 24$	Example: $-3x^5 + 4x^3 - 2x^2 + 24$

The multiplicity of a root

A root $x = r$ of a polynomial $p(x)$ of degree n has multiplicity k $(k \leq n)$ if k is the biggest number such that $(x - r)^k$ is a factor of $p(x)$. A root of multiplicity 1 is called a simple root.

(a) If k is **even**, then the graph touches (bounces off) the x-axis at $x = r$ but does not cross it.	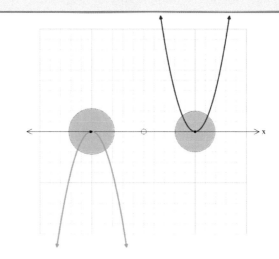
(b) If $k = 1$ (simple root), then the graph crosses the x-axis at $x = r$.	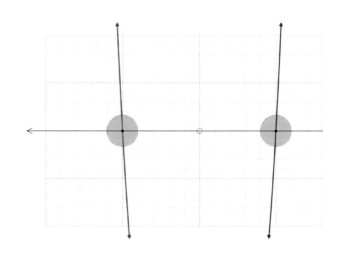
(c) If k is **odd and greater than 1**, then the graph crosses the x-axis at $x = r$ and has an inflection point there.	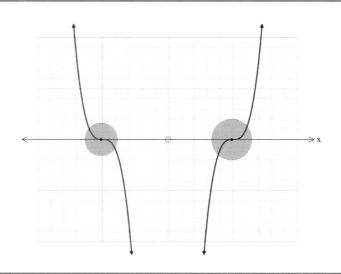

Sequences, Series and Binomial theorem

A **sequence** is a set of numbers arranged in a definite order.

$$a_1, a_2, a_3, \ldots, a_n, \ldots$$

where $a_1, a_2, a_3, \ldots, a_n, \ldots$ are called **terms**.

Arithmetic Sequence and Series

A sequence $\{a_n\}$ in which each term differs from the previous one by the same constant d (common difference) is called **arithmetic sequence**.

$$a_{n+1} - a_n = d$$

The general term a_n can be found using the formula

$$a_n = a_1 + (n-1)d$$

The Sum (S_n) of the first n terms of an arithmetic sequence $\{a_n\}$ is called **arithmetic series** and given by

$$S_n = \frac{n}{2}(a_1 + a_n)$$

$$S_n = \frac{n}{2}[2a_1 + (n-1)d]$$

Note: If we want to deduce the general term a_n from S_n, we can use the following formula:

$$a_n = S_n - S_{n-1} \text{ and } a_1 = S_1$$

Example

An arithmetic sequence has a 1st term of 80 and a 24th term of 172. Find the 74th term, an expression for the general term and the sum S_n.

Solution

Using the formula $a_n = a_1 + (n-1)d$, we have that

$$a_{24} = a_1 + (24-1)d \Rightarrow d = \frac{172-80}{23} = \frac{92}{23} = 4$$

Thus, $a_{74} = a_1 + (74-1)d = 80 + 73 \times 4 = 372$

The general term is $a_n = 80 + (n-1)4$

and the sum of the first n terms is $S_n = \frac{n}{2}[160 + (n-1)4]$

Geometric Sequence and Series

A sequence $\{a_n\}$ in which each term can be obtained from the previous one by multiplying a non-zero constant r (common ratio) is called **geometric sequence**.

$$\frac{a_{n+1}}{a_n} = r$$

The general term a_n can be found using the formula

$$a_n = a_1 r^{n-1}$$

The Sum (S_n) of the first n terms of a geometric sequence $\{a_n\}$ is called **geometric series** and is given by

$$S_n = \frac{a_1(r^n - 1)}{r - 1}$$

The Sum to infinity (S_∞) of geometric series is given by

$$S_\infty = \frac{a_1}{1 - r}, |r| < 1 \ (-1 < r < 1)$$

If a geometric sequence has a finite sum ($|r| < 1$) then it is called **convergent**. Otherwise, it is called **divergent**.

Example

A geometric sequence has a 4th term of 32 and a 7th term of 256. Find the 10th term, an expression for the general term $\boldsymbol{a_n}$ and the sum $\boldsymbol{S_n}$.

Solution: Using the formula $\boldsymbol{a_n = a_1 r^{n-1}}$ we have that

$$a_4 = a_1 r^{4-1} \Leftrightarrow 32 = a_1 r^3$$

$$a_7 = a_1 r^{7-1} \Leftrightarrow 256 = a_1 r^6$$

Dividing the two equations, we have that $\frac{a_1 r^3}{a_1 r^6} = \frac{32}{256} \Leftrightarrow r^3 = 8 \Leftrightarrow r = 2$

and $32 = a_1 r^3 \Leftrightarrow 32 = a_1 2^3 \Leftrightarrow a_1 = 4$

Thus, $a_{10} = a_1 r^{n-1} = 4 \times 2^{10-1} = 2048$

The general term is $\boldsymbol{a_n = 4 \times 2^{n-1}}$ and the sum is $\boldsymbol{S_n = \frac{4(2^n - 1)}{2-1} = 4(2^n - 1)}$

Sigma Notation

> Sigma notation is a way of expressing sums uses the Greek letter Σ
>
> $$\sum_{i=1}^{n} a_i = a_1 + a_2 + \cdots + a_n$$
>
> Where i is the index of summation taking values from 1 to n.

Properties of Sigma Notation

$\sum_{i=1}^{n}(a_i \pm b_i) = \sum_{i=1}^{n} a_i \pm \sum_{i=1}^{n} b_i$	$\sum_{i=1}^{n} c a_i = c \sum_{i=1}^{n} a_i$
$\sum_{i=1}^{n} c = cn$	$\sum_{i=k}^{n} a_i = \sum_{i=1}^{n} a_i - \sum_{i=1}^{k-1} a_i$

Binomial Theorem

> $$(a+b)^n = a^n + \binom{n}{1} a^{n-1} b + \ldots + \binom{n}{r} a^{n-r} b^r + \cdots + b^n = \sum_{k=0}^{n} \binom{n}{k} a^{n-k} b^k$$
>
> where $\binom{n}{r} = \frac{n!}{r!(n-r)!}$ and $n!$ is the product of the first n positive integers for $n \geq 1$
>
> $$n! = 1 \times 2 \times 3 \times \cdots \times n \text{ and } 0! = 1$$

Properties of the symbol $\binom{n}{r}$

$$\binom{n}{0} = 1 \qquad \binom{n}{1} = n \qquad \binom{n}{n} = 1 \qquad \binom{n}{r} = \binom{n}{n-r}$$

Pascal's Triangle {Blaise Pascal (1623 –1662)}

The Pascal's triangle is a triangular arrangement of numbers that gives the coefficients in the expansion of any binomial expression, such as $(a + b)^n$.

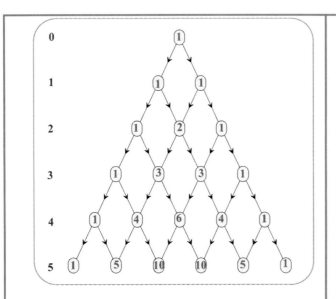

The first row is one 1. Then we have two 1s. The outsides of the triangle are always 1, but the insides are different. To find the number on the next row, add the two numbers above it together. Every row is built from the row above it.

For example the expansion of $(a + b)^3$ according to Pascal's Triangle will be
$$(a + b)^3 = 1a^3 + 3a^2b + 3ab^2 + 1b^3$$

Examples

1. Using the binomial theorem, expand $(3x + 1)^4$.

Solution

Using the formula
$$(a + b)^n = a^n + \binom{n}{1} a^{n-1}b + \cdots + \binom{n}{r} a^{n-r}b^r + \cdots + b^n$$
we have that

$$(3x + 1)^4 = (3x)^4 + \binom{4}{1}(3x)^{4-1}1 + \binom{4}{2}(3x)^{4-2}1 + \binom{4}{3}(3x)^{4-3}1 + 1^4 =$$
$$= 81x^4 + 108x^3 + 54x^2 + 12x + 1$$

2. Find the term in x^3 in the expansion of $\left(4x - \dfrac{5}{x^2}\right)^6$

Solution

The general term of this binomial expansion is given by the following formula:

$$\binom{6}{r}(4x)^{6-r}\left(\frac{-5}{x^2}\right)^r = \binom{6}{r}4^{6-r}x^{6-r}(-5)^r\left(\frac{1}{x^2}\right)^r = \binom{6}{r}4^{6-r}(-5)^r x^{6-r}(x^{-2})^r =$$

$$= \binom{6}{r}4^{6-r}(-5)^r x^{6-r}x^{-2r} = \binom{6}{r}4^{6-r}(-5)^r x^{6-3r}$$

Since we have to find the term in x^3, we set

$$6 - 3r = 3$$

$$r = 1$$

Therefore the coefficient of x^3 is $\binom{6}{1}4^{6-1}(-5)^1 = 6 \cdot 4^5 \cdot (-5) = -30720$

Note: A useful hint concerning the factorial notation is that, for example, we can express 7! as $5! \times 6 \times 7$ instead of $7! = 1 \times 2 \times 3 \times 4 \times 5 \times 6 \times 7$

Compound Interest

The compound interest formula for calculating the **Future Value** (**FV**) of an amount with a **Present Value** (**PV**) is:

$$FV = PV\left(1 + \frac{r}{100k}\right)^{kn}$$

where r is the nominal annual interest rate, n the number of years and k is the number of compounding periods per year.

Example

Gregory invests \$80,000 in a savings account, earning 5% per year compounded monthly.

Calculate the value of the investment after 4 complete years.

Answer

In this example, r $= 5, n = 4$ and $k = 12$

$$FV = PV\left(1 + \frac{r}{100k}\right)^{kn} = \$80,000\left(1 + \frac{5}{100 \times 12}\right)^{12\times4} = \$97,671.63 = \$97,700 \ (3 \ s.f.)$$

Mathematical Induction

The principle of Mathematical Induction

The steps in proving a statement by mathematical induction are the following:

1. Check that the statement is true for an initial value (usually $n = 1$). **(Base case)**

2. Prove that if the statement is true for any positive integer $n = k$, then it is also true for the next integer $n = k + 1$. **(Inductive step)**

Once these steps are completed, the statement holds for all positive integers n.

Examples

1. Prove that $2^n > n^2$ for all natural numbers $n \geq 5$.

Solution

- First, we check that $2^5 = 32 > 5^2 = 25$, so the inequality is true for $n = 5$.
- Assume true for $n = k$ i.e. $2^k > k^2$ for any integer $k \geq 5$.
- Then $2^{k+1} = 2 \cdot 2^k > 2 \cdot k^2 > (k + 1)^2$

The last inequality holds since $2k^2 - (k + 1)^2 = k^2 - 2k - 1 > 0 , k \geq 5$

Since the inequality is true for $n = 5$, and it was also proved that if the inequality is true for $n = k$ it is also true for $n = k + 1$, it follows by the principle of mathematical induction that the inequality is true for all positive integers n.

2. Prove for $n \geq 1$ that

$$\sum_{r=1}^{n} rr! = (n+1)! - 1$$

Solution

▫ First, we check that

$$LHS: \sum_{r=1}^{1} rr! = 1 \cdot 1! = 1$$

$$RHS: (1+1)! - 1 = 2 - 1 = 1$$

so the inequality is true for $n = 1$

▫ Assume true for $n = k$

i.e.

$$\sum_{r=1}^{k} rr! = (k+1)! - 1$$

for any integer $k \geq 1$

▫ We need to prove

$$\sum_{r=1}^{k+1} rr! = (k+2)! - 1$$

$$\sum_{r=1}^{k+1} rr! = \sum_{r=1}^{k} rr! + (k+1) \cdot (k+1)! = (k+1)! - 1 + (k+1) \cdot (k+1)! =$$

$$= (k+1)! - 1 + (k+1) \cdot (k+1)! = (k+1)! (1 + k + 1) - 1 = (k+2)! - 1 \text{ Q.E.D. (Quod Erat}$$

Demonstrandum).

Since the proposition is true for $n = 1$, and it was also proved that if the proposition is true for $n = k$ it

is also true for $n = k + 1$, it follows by the principle of mathematical induction that the proposition is true

for all positive integers n.

Functions

Relation: A relation is any set of ordered-pair numbers.

For example, let the relation $R = \{(1,15),(2,17),(3,18),(4,26),(4,67)\}$

The set of all first elements is called the **domain** of the relation.
   The domain of R is the set $\{1,2,3,4\}$

The set of second elements is called the **range** of the relation.
   The range of R is the set $\{15,17,18,26,67\}$

Function: A function is a relation in which **no** two ordered pairs have the same first element.

A function associates each element in its domain with **one and only one** element in its range.

All functions are relations, but not all relations are functions.

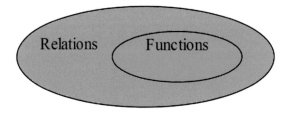

Example

Determine whether the following relations are functions

a) $A = \{(0,5),(3,7),(6,9),(8,15)\}$
b) $B = \{(10,13),(10,31),(20,15),(41,23)\}$

Answer

 a) $A = \{(0,5),(3,7),(6,9),(8,15)\}$ is a function because all the first elements are different.

b) $B = \{(10,13),(10,31),(20,15),(41,23)\}$ is not a function because the first element, 10, is repeated.

The **domain (D_f) of a function f** is the set of all allowable values of the independent variable, commonly known as the x-values.

1. You cannot have negative under a square root or any even radical.
2. You cannot have zero in the denominator.
3. You cannot have a negative number or zero as an argument of a logarithmic function.
4. You cannot have a negative number or zero or one as the base of a logarithmic function.

The **range (R_f)** of a **function f** is the set of y-values when all x-values in the domain are evaluated into the function.

▨ A function $f(x)$ is **even** if $f(-x) = f(x)$ for all $x \in D_f$. An **even** function is symmetric with respect to the **y-axis**.

▨ A function $f(x)$ is **odd** if $f(-x) = -f(x)$ for all $x \in D_f$. An **odd** function has rotational symmetry with respect to the **origin**.

Note: The only function that is both **even** and **odd** is the function $f(x) = 0$.

Vertical Line Test

The vertical line test is a method to determine if a relation is a function. A relation is a function if any vertical line intersects the graph in at most one point.

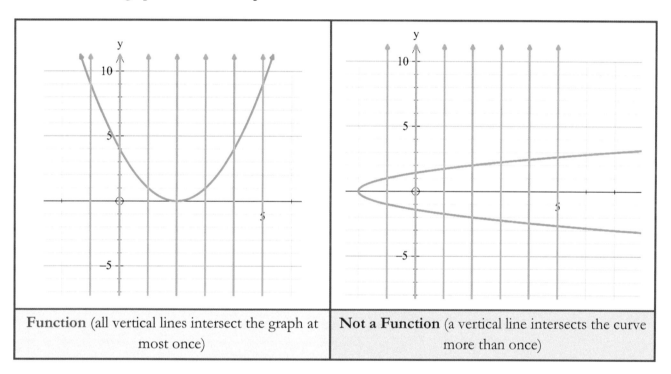

| Function (all vertical lines intersect the graph at most once) | Not a Function (a vertical line intersects the curve more than once) |

Inverse Function

The inverse of the function f is denoted by f^{-1} and is pronounced "f inverse" and <u>it's not</u> the reciprocal of f $\left(f^{-1}(x) \neq \frac{1}{f(x)}\right)$.

To determine algebraically the formula for the inverse of a function $y = f(x)$, you switch y and x to get $x = f(y)$ and then solve for y to get $y = f^{-1}(x)$.

Example

Find the inverse function of $f(x) = \dfrac{2x+3}{x-5}$

Solution

$$y = \frac{2x+3}{x-5}$$ Replace $f(x)$ by y

$$x = \frac{2y+3}{y-5}$$ Switch the x's and y

$$x(y-5) = 2y+3$$ Solve for y

$$xy - 5x = 2y + 3$$

$$xy - 2y = 5x + 3$$

$$y(x-2) = 5x + 3$$

$$y = \frac{5x+3}{x-2}$$

$$f^{-1}(x) = \frac{5x+3}{x-2}$$ Replace y with $f^{-1}(x)$

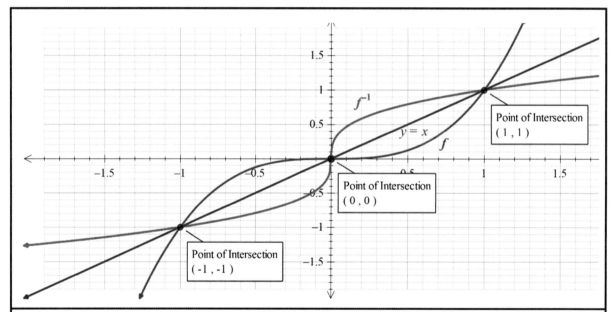

The inverse of a function differs from the function in that all the x-coordinates and y-coordinates have been switched. That is, if for example (4,9) is a point on the graph of the function, then the point (9,4) lies on the graph of the inverse function.

The graph of a function and its inverse are mirror images of each other. They are reflected in the identity function $y = x$.

Important: If the graphs of a function and its inverse intersect at one point, then this point will be on the line $y = x$, as shown in the figure above. Therefore, if we want to find the point(s) of intersection between $f(x)$ and $f^{-1}(x)$, instead of finding $f^{-1}(x)$ and then equating both of the functions, we could set $f(x) = x$ and find the common points between $f(x)$ and $y = x$.

Note: A function is said to be a **self-inverse** if $f(x) = f^{-1}(x)$ for all x in the domain.

For example, the reciprocal function $f(x) = \frac{1}{x}, (x \neq 0)$ is self-inverse.

Notes: The domain of f^{-1} is equal to the range of f.

The range of f^{-1} is equal to the domain of f.

For example, if $f(4) = 9$ then $f^{-1}(9) = 4$

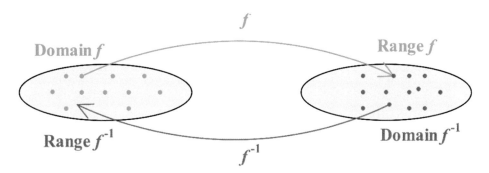

Existence of an Inverse Function

If the function has an inverse that is also a function, then there can only be one y for every x.

A **one-to-one** function is a function in which for every x there is exactly one y and for every y, there is exactly one x. For $f(x)$ to have an **inverse function,** it must be **one-to-one.**

Some functions do not have inverse functions. For example, consider $f(x) = x^2$. This is not an one-to-one function since there are two numbers that f takes to 1, $f(1) = 1$ and $f(-1) = 1$.

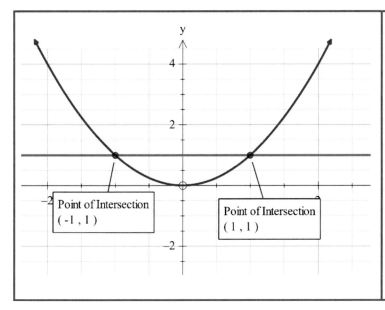

One way to check if a function is one-to-one is the **Horizontal Line Test.**

If a horizontal line intersects the graph of the function more than once, then the function is not one-to-one.

If no horizontal line intersects the graph of the function more than once, then the function is one-to-one.

For example the function $f(x) = x^2$ is not one-to-one since the line $y = 1$ intersects the graph of the function twice.

Composite functions

If we have two functions $f(x)$ and $g(x)$, we can define a composite function

$$(f \circ g)(x) = f(g(x))$$

If a function f has also an inverse then

$$(f \circ f^{-1})(x) = (f^{-1} \circ f)(x) = x$$

where $I(x) = x$ is the identity function.

Example: Given $f(x) = 2x + 3$ and $g(x) = x^2 + 4$, find $f \circ g, g \circ f, f \circ f$ and $g \circ g$.

Solution:

$$(f \circ g)(x) = f\big(g(x)\big) = f(x^2 + 4) = 2(x^2 + 4) + 3$$

$$(g \circ f)(x) = g\big(f(x)\big) = g(2x + 3) = (2x + 3)^2 + 4$$

$$(f \circ f)(x) = f\big(f(x)\big) = f(2x + 3) = 2(2x + 3) + 3$$

$$(g \circ g)(x) = g\big(g(x)\big) = g(x^2 + 4) = (x^2 + 4)^2 + 4$$

Example: The function f is defined by $f(x) = x^3 + 4$.

Find an expression for $g(x)$ in terms of x given that $(f \circ g)(x) = x - 2.$

Solution: If $f(x) = x^3 + 4$ then $f^{-1}(x) = \sqrt[3]{x - 4}$.

If $h(x) = x - 2$ then we have to find a function g such that

$$(f \circ g)(x) = h(x) \Rightarrow \left(\overbrace{f^{-1} \circ f}^{x} \circ g \right)(x) = (f^{-1} \circ h)(x) \Rightarrow$$

$$\Rightarrow (x \circ g)(x) = (f^{-1} \circ h)(x) \Rightarrow g(x) = f^{-1}(h(x)) \Rightarrow g(x) = f^{-1}(x - 2)$$

$$\Rightarrow g(x) = \sqrt[3]{(x - 2) - 4} \Rightarrow g(x) = \sqrt[3]{x - 6}$$

Asymptotes

Horizontal Asymptote

A **Horizontal Asymptote** is a horizontal line that the graph of a function approaches, as x approaches negative or positive infinity. A horizontal asymptote may intersect the graph of the function.

For the following example (Graph 1) the function f has a horizontal asymptote at $y = -1$ and the function g has a horizontal asymptote at $y = 1$.

$$\lim_{x \to \infty} f(x) = -1$$

$$\lim_{x \to -\infty} g(x) = 1$$

Vertical Asymptote

A **Vertical Asymptote** of a curve is a line of the form $x = a$ such that as x approaches some constant value a then the curve goes towards infinity (positive or negative). <u>A vertical asymptote doesn't intersect the graph of the function</u> (Graph 2).

For the following example (Graph 2) the function f has a vertical asymptote at $x = 1$ and a horizontal asymptote at $y = 0$.

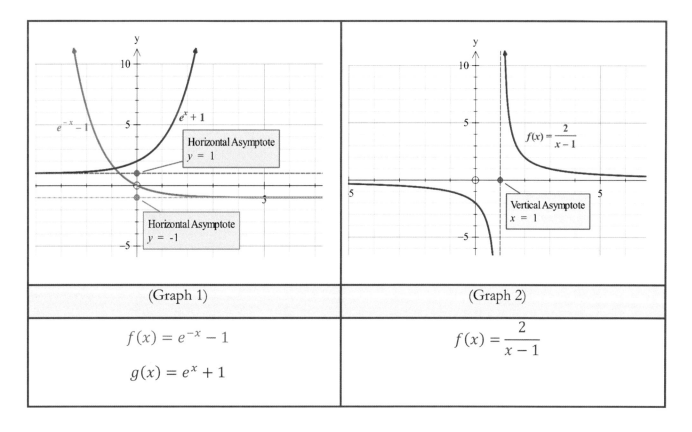

(Graph 1)	(Graph 2)
$f(x) = e^{-x} - 1$ $g(x) = e^{x} + 1$	$f(x) = \dfrac{2}{x - 1}$

Rational Functions and Asymptotes

Let f be a rational function

$$f(x) = \frac{a_n x^n + \cdots + a_1 x + a_0}{b_m x^m + \cdots + b_1 x + b_0}$$

The graph of $y = f(x)$ will have **vertical asymptotes** at those values of x for which the denominator is equal to zero.

The graph of $y = f(x)$ may have a horizontal asymptote according to the following:

- If the degree of the numerator is larger than the degree of the denominator $(n > m)$ then there is <u>no</u> horizontal asymptote.

- If the degree of the numerator is equal to the degree of the denominator $(n = m)$ then the graph of $y = f(x)$ will have a horizontal asymptote at $y = \frac{a_n}{b_m}$.

- If the degree of the numerator is less than the degree of the denominator $(n < m)$ then the graph of $y = f(x)$ will have a horizontal asymptote at $y = 0$ (x-axis).

Oblique asymptote (Optional)

Finally, if the degree of the numerator differs from the smaller denominator degree by 1, then there is an **oblique (or slant) asymptote** that is the line described by the quotient of the numerator divided by the denominator. The oblique asymptotes can be found by using polynomial division, where the quotient is the equation of the oblique asymptote.

Examples

1. The function

$$f(x) = \frac{x - 2}{x + 3}$$

has a **vertical asymptote** at $x = -3$ and a horizontal asymptote at $y = 1$.

2. The function

$$f(x) = \frac{x^2 + 4}{x + 2}$$

has a **vertical asymptote** at $x = -2$, has not any horizontal asymptote and has an **oblique asymptote** $y = x - 2$ since the quotient of the division $(x^2 + 4) : (x + 2)$ is $x - 2$.

3. The function

$$f(x) = \frac{x - 2}{x^2 + 3}$$

has not any **vertical asymptote** and has a horizontal asymptote $y = 0$.

4.   The function

$$f(x) = \frac{x^2 - 5x + 6}{(x - 2)(3x + 4)}$$

has a **vertical asymptote** at $x = -\frac{4}{3}$ only and a horizontal asymptote at $y = \frac{1}{3}$.

This rational function has **<u>no</u>** vertical asymptote at $x = 2$, since the function f can be written as

$$f(x) = \frac{\cancel{(x - 2)}(x - 3)}{\cancel{(x - 2)}(3x + 4)} = \frac{(x - 3)}{(3x + 4)}$$

Important: If $x - a$ is a factor of both the numerator and denominator of a rational function, then there is a missing point (**hole**) in the graph of the function where $x = a$. Thus, the value $x = a$ is <u>not an x −intercept</u> and <u>there is not a vertical asymptote</u> at $x = a$.

Graph Transformation of Functions

Horizontal Translations

A horizontal translation means that every point (x, y) on the graph of the original function $f(x)$ is transformed to $(x + c, y)$, $(x - c, y)$ on the graph of the transformed function $f(x - c)$ or $f(x + c)$ respectively, where c is a **positive** constant.

The graph of $f(x - c)$ is shifted **right** c units (Graph 1).

The graph of $f(x + c)$ is shifted **left** c units (Graph 2).

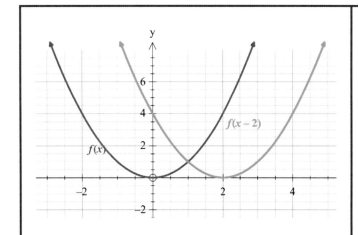	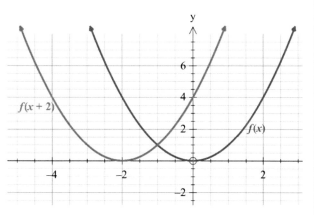
(Graph 1)	(Graph 2)
Horizontal shift 2 units to the **right**	Horizontal shift 2 units to the **left**
$f(x) \rightarrow f(x - 2)$	$f(x + 2) \leftarrow f(x)$
$(0, 0) \rightarrow (2, 0)$	$(-2, 0) \leftarrow (0, 0)$

Vertical Translations

If $f(x)$ is the original function and $c > 0$ then

the graph of $f(x) + c$ is shifted **up c** units (Graph 3)

and the graph of $f(x) - c$ is shifted **down c** units (Graph 4).

A vertical translation means that every point (x, y) on the graph of the original function $f(x)$ is transformed
to $(x, y + c)$, $(x, y - c)$ on the graph of the transformed function $f(x) + c$ or $f(x) - c$ respectively.

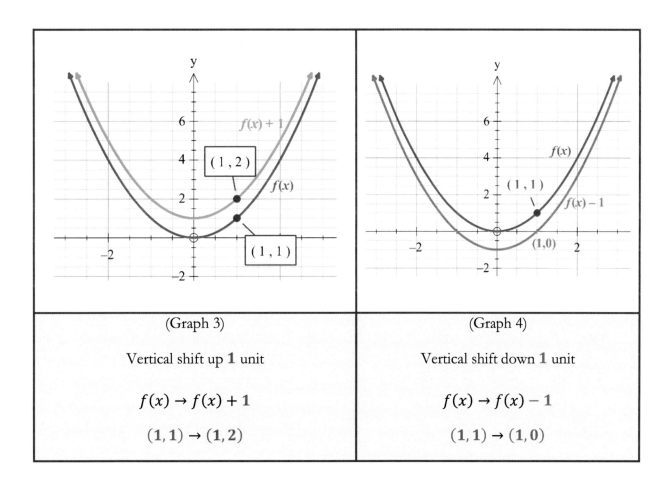

(Graph 3)	(Graph 4)
Vertical shift up **1** unit	Vertical shift down **1** unit
$f(x) \rightarrow f(x) + 1$	$f(x) \rightarrow f(x) - 1$
$(1, 1) \rightarrow (1, 2)$	$(1, 1) \rightarrow (1, 0)$

Note: Sometimes, the horizontal and vertical translations are denoted as a vector. For example translation
by the vector $\binom{-1}{4}$ denotes a horizontal shift of 1 unit to the left, and vertical shift of 4 units up.

Vertical Stretching and Shrinking (Dilations)

If $f(x)$ is the original function and $a \in \mathbb{R}$ then the graph of $af(x)$ is a **vertical stretch** by **a scale factor of a** (Graph 5).

A vertical stretch means that every point (x, y) on the graph of the original function $f(x)$ is transformed to (x, ay) on the graph of the transformed function $af(x)$.

Horizontal Stretching and Shrinking (Dilations)

If $f(x)$ is the original function and $a \in \mathbb{R}$ then the graph of $f(ax)$ is a **horizontal stretch** by **a scale factor of $\frac{1}{a}$** (Graph 6).

A horizontal stretch means that every point (x, y) on the graph of the original function $f(x)$ is transformed to $(\frac{x}{a}, y)$ on the graph of the transformed function $f(ax)$.

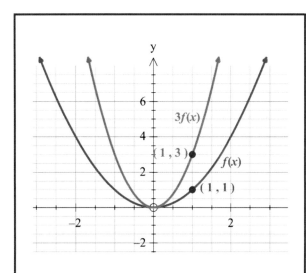

(Graph 5)

Vertical Stretch by a scale factor of **3**

$$f(x) \rightarrow 3f(x)$$

$$(1, 1) \rightarrow (1, 3)$$

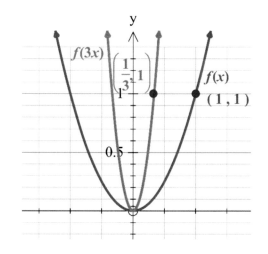

(Graph 6)

Horizontal Stretch by a scale factor of $\frac{1}{3}$

$$f(x) \rightarrow f(3x)$$

$$(1, 1) \rightarrow \left(\frac{1}{3}, 1\right)$$

Reflections

If $f(x)$ is the original function then

the graph of $-f(x)$ is a **reflection in the x-axis** (Graph 7).

and the graph of $f(-x)$ is a **reflection in the y-axis** (Graph 8).

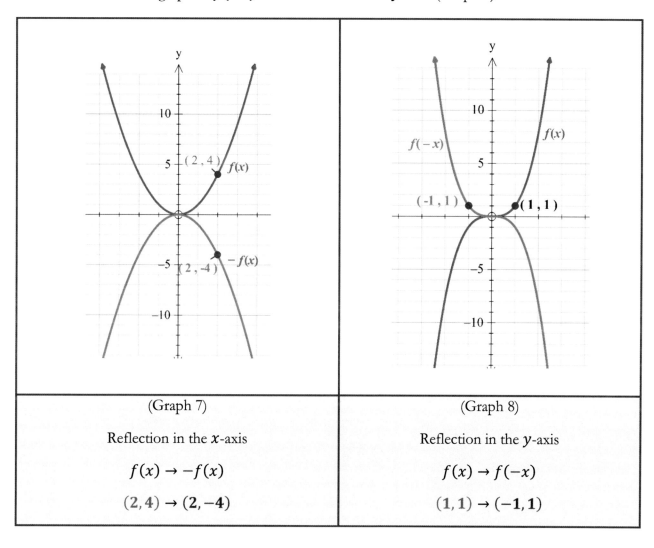

(Graph 7)	(Graph 8)
Reflection in the x-axis	Reflection in the y-axis
$f(x) \rightarrow -f(x)$	$f(x) \rightarrow f(-x)$
$(2, 4) \rightarrow (2, -4)$	$(1, 1) \rightarrow (-1, 1)$

Absolute Value Transformations

Every part of the graph which is below x-axis, is reflected in x-axis. (Graph 11)

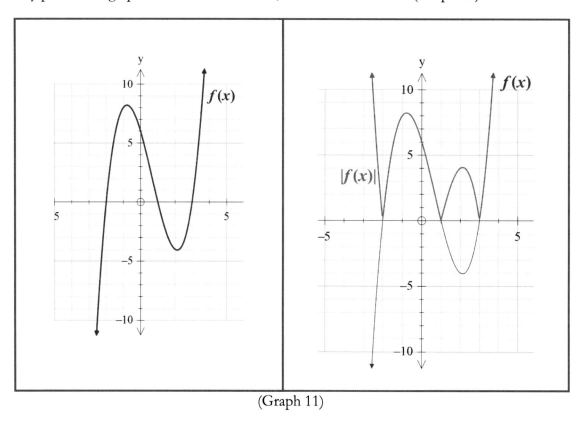

(Graph 11)

For $x \geq 0$ the graph is exactly the same as this of the original function. (Graph 12)

For $x < 0$ the graph is a reflection of the graph for $x \geq 0$ in the y-axis. (Graph 12)

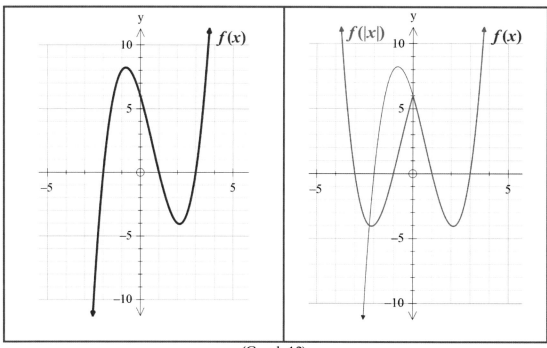

(Graph 12)

Order of Transformations

When we perform multiple transformations, the order of these transformations may affect the final graph. Apart from a few exceptions, the intended order could be the following:

1. Horizontal Shifts

2. Stretch / Shrink

3. Reflections

4. Vertical Shifts

Example

How can we obtain the graph of $g(x) = 3\sqrt{2x - 1}$ from the graph of $f(x) = \sqrt{x}$?

Answer

The order of the transformations could be the following:

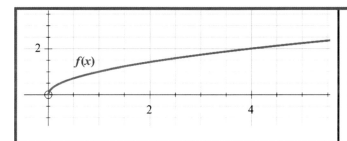

$$f(x) = \sqrt{x}$$

For example, the point $(4,2)$ will be transformed as follows

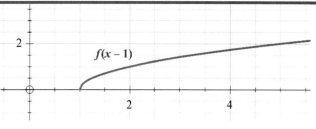

$$f(x - 1) = \sqrt{x - 1}$$

Horizontal Shift 1 unit to the right

$$(4,2) \to (5,2)$$

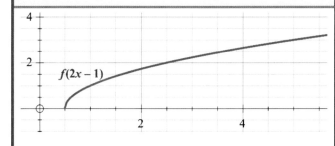

$$f(2x - 1) = \sqrt{2x - 1}$$

Horizontal Shrink by a scale factor of $\frac{1}{2}$

$$(5,2) \to \left(\frac{5}{2}, 2\right)$$

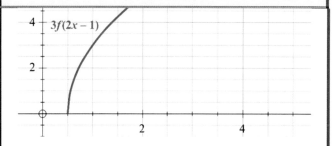

$$3f(2x - 1) = 3\sqrt{2x - 1}$$

Vertical Stretch by a scale factor of 3

$$\left(\frac{5}{2}, 2\right) \to \left(\frac{5}{2}, 6\right)$$

Graph of the reciprocal of a function $\left(\dfrac{1}{f(x)}\right)$

The following guidelines are useful in order to sketch the reciprocal of a function given the graph of the original function:

1. Where $f(x)$ is **positive** or **negative** then $\dfrac{1}{f(x)}$ is also **positive** or **negative** respectively.

2. Where $f(x)$ has **zero(s)** then the reciprocal function $\dfrac{1}{f(x)}$ has **vertical asymptote(s)** and vice versa.

3. Where $f(x)$ has a **horizontal asymptote** at $y = c$ then the reciprocal function $\dfrac{1}{f(x)}$ has also horizontal asymptote at $y = \dfrac{1}{c}$.

4. Where the original function $f(x)$ is **increasing** then the reciprocal function $\dfrac{1}{f(x)}$ is **decreasing**.

5. Where the original function $f(x)$ is **decreasing** then the reciprocal function $\dfrac{1}{f(x)}$ is **increasing**.

6. If the original function $f(x)$ has a **maximum** at $(c, f(c))$ then the reciprocal function $\dfrac{1}{f(x)}$ has a **minimum** at $\left(c, \dfrac{1}{f(c)}\right)$.

7. If the original function $f(x)$ has a **minimum** at $(c, f(c))$ then the reciprocal function $\dfrac{1}{f(x)}$ has a **maximum** at $\left(c, \dfrac{1}{f(c)}\right)$.

8. If the original function $f(x)$ has a **point of inflection** at $(c, f(c))$ then the reciprocal function $\dfrac{1}{f(x)}$ has also a **point of inflection** at $\left(c, \dfrac{1}{f(c)}\right)$.

Example

1. How can we obtain the graph of $\dfrac{1}{f(x)}$ from the graph of $f(x)$ given below?

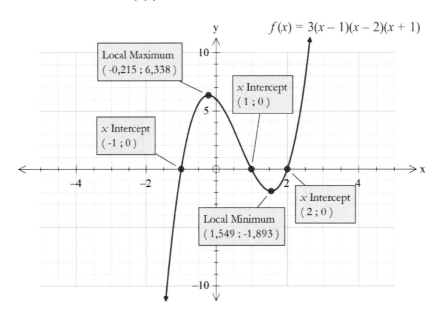

Answer

The graph of the reciprocal function $\frac{1}{f(x)}$ has 3 vertical asymptotes at $x = -1$, $x = 1$ and $x = 2$ which are the points where the original function $f(x)$ has x-intercepts (zeros).

The maximum point of $f(x)$ at $(-0.215, 6.34)$ becomes a minimum point of the reciprocal function $\frac{1}{f(x)}$ with coordinates $\left(-0.215, \frac{1}{6.34}\right)$.

The minimum point of $f(x)$ at $(1.55, -1.90)$ becomes a maximum point of the reciprocal function $\frac{1}{f(x)}$ with coordinates $\left(1.55, -\frac{1}{1.90}\right)$.

Where $f(x)$ is **positive** or **negative** then $\frac{1}{f(x)}$ is also **positive** or **negative** respectively.

Where the original function $f(x)$ is **increasing** then the reciprocal function $\frac{1}{f(x)}$ is **decreasing**.

Where the original function $f(x)$ is **decreasing** then the reciprocal function $\frac{1}{f(x)}$ is **increasing**.

Therefore the graphs of the reciprocal function $\frac{1}{f(x)}$ and this one of $f(x)$ are shown on the following diagram. (Graph 13)

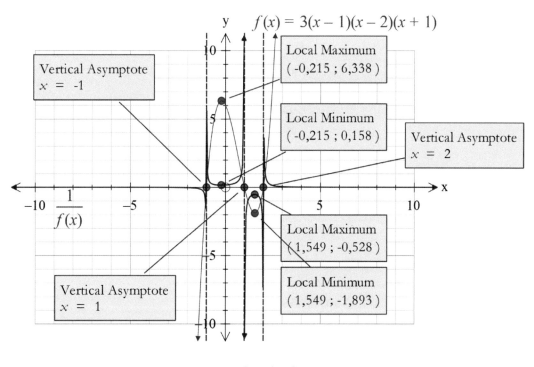

(Graph 13)

Exponential & Logarithmic Functions

Exponential Function

An Exponential function is a function of the form $f(x) = a^x$ where a is a positive constant and $a \neq 1$.

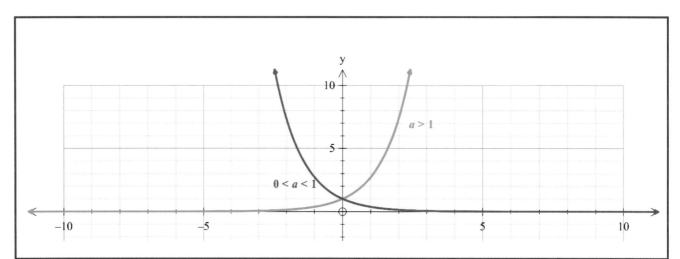

If $a > 1$ then the exponential function increases	If $0 < a < 1$ then the exponential function decreases

In either case, the x-axis is its horizontal asymptote

The domain of $f(x) = a^x$ consists of all real numbers and its range consists of positive numbers only.

Laws of Exponents

If a, b are positive numbers, x, y are real numbers and m, n are positive integers then:

$a^{x+y} = a^x a^y$	$\left(\dfrac{a}{b}\right)^x = \dfrac{a^x}{b^x}$	$a^{\frac{m}{n}} = \sqrt[n]{a^m}$
$a^{x-y} = \dfrac{a^x}{a^y}$	$a^0 = 1$	$a^{\frac{1}{n}} = \sqrt[n]{a}$
$(a^x)^y = a^{xy}$	$a^{-x} = \dfrac{1}{a^x}$	
$(ab)^x = a^x b^x$	$a^x = \dfrac{1}{a^{-x}}$	

Note: To solve exponential equations without using logarithms, you need to have equations with the same base to some other power

For example: $2^{x+3} = 2^{3x+5}$ then $x + 3 = 3x + 5 \Rightarrow 2x = -2 \Rightarrow x = -1$.

Logarithmic Function

The inverse of the exponential function $f(x) = a^x$ is the logarithmic function with base a

$$f^{-1}(x) = log_a x, \text{ where } a, x > 0 \text{ and } a \neq 1$$

If $0 < a < 1$ then the logarithmic function decreases.

If $a > 1$ then the logarithmic function increases.

In either case, the y-axis is its **vertical asymptote.**

Domain: $x > 0$
Range: $y \in \mathbb{R}$

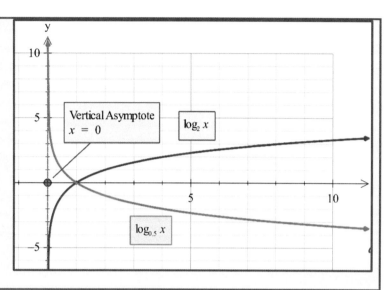

The graph of
$$f(x) = log_a x$$
can be obtained by reflecting the graph of
$$g(x) = a^x$$
across the line $y = x$ since they **are inverse to each other**.

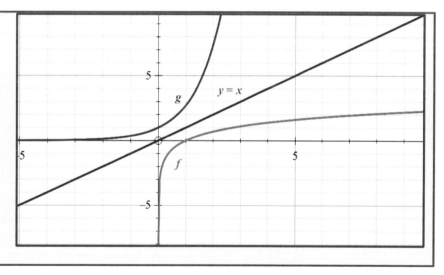

$$log_a x = y \iff a^y = x$$

$$log_a a^x = x \text{ for every } x \in \mathbb{R}$$

$$a^{log_a x} = x \text{ for every } x > 0$$

$$log_a 1 = 0$$

$$log_a a = 1$$

The logarithm with base e is referred to as a **natural logarithm** $log_e x \equiv lnx$ where e is the [1]Euler's number which is defined as $e = \lim_{n \to \infty} \left(1 + \frac{1}{n}\right)^n = 2.71828..$

[1]{Leonhard Euler (1707 –1783)}

Laws of Logarithms

If a, b are positive numbers, $a, b \neq 1$ and x, y are real positive numbers, and k is a real number then:

- $log_a(xy) = log_a x + log_a y$

- $log_a\left(\frac{x}{y}\right) = log_a x - log_a y$

- $log_a\left(\frac{1}{y}\right) = -log_a y$

- $log_a x^k = k log_a x$

- $log_a x = \frac{log_b x}{log_b a}$ (change of base)

- $a^{log b} = b^{log a}$

Solving Logarithmic equations containing only logarithms

If an equation contains only two logarithms, on opposite sides of the equal sign, with the same base and both with a coefficient of one, then we can just drop the logarithms.

$$log_a x = log_a y$$

then

$$x = y$$

Important: Use only solutions that are in the intersection of the domains of the logarithmic terms. We need to make sure that when we plug our solutions back into the original equation, we get a positive number. Otherwise, we must reject these solutions.

Example

$$log_3(x + 3) = log_3(2x - 5)$$

$$x + 3 = 2x - 5$$

$$x = 8$$

We plug this solution back into the original equation, and we get a positive number, so it is accepted.

Solving Logarithmic Equations Containing Terms without Logarithms

We simplify the problem using the properties of logarithms and then rewrite the logarithmic problem in exponential form.

Example Solve the logarithmic equation
$$log_3(x+3) = 4$$

Solution

$$log_3(x+3) = 4$$
$$x + 3 = 3^4$$
$$x = 81 - 3 = 78$$

Solving Exponential Equations using Logarithms

We simplify the problem using the properties of logarithms and then rewrite the exponential problem in logarithmic form.

Example Solve the exponential equation
$$2^{x-3} = 15$$

Solution

$$2^{x-3} = 15$$

$$log_2 2^{x-3} = log_2 15$$

$$(x-3)log_2 2 = log_2 15$$

$$(x-3)1 = log_2 15$$

$$x = log_2 15 + 3$$

Example The number of bacteria in a colony, B, is modeled by the function $B(t) = 500 \times 3^{0.1t}$ where t is measured in days.
(a) Find the initial number of bacteria in this colony.
(b) Find the number of bacteria after 10 days.
(c) How long does it take for the number of bacteria in the colony to reach 2000?

Solution

(a) $B(0) = 500 \times 3^{0.1 \times 0} = 500$
(b) $B(10) = 500 \times 3^{0.1 \times 10} = 500 \times 3 = 1500$
(c) $B(t) = 500 \times 3^{0.1t} = 2000 \Rightarrow 3^{0.1t} = 4 \Rightarrow 0.1t ln3 = ln4 \Rightarrow t = \frac{ln4}{0.1 ln3} = 12.6$ days

Trigonometry

Degrees - Radians measurement of angles

$$2\pi\ radians = 360^o\ degrees$$

Circle Sectors and Segments

A **sector** of a circle is a region of a circle bounded by a central angle and its intercepted arc.
The region of a circle bounded by an arc and a chord is called a **segment** of a circle.

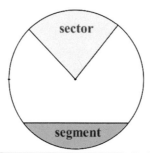

Arc length L	Sector Area
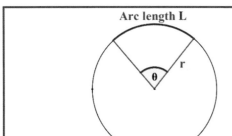	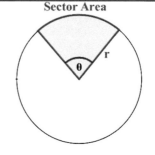
Arc Length: $L = \theta r$ θ: in radians	**Sector Area:** $A = \frac{1}{2}\theta r^2$ θ: in radians
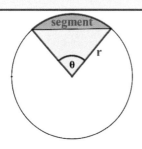	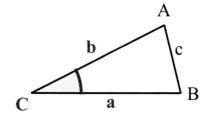
Area of the segment = Area of the sector - Area of the triangle = $\frac{1}{2}\theta r^2 - \frac{1}{2}r^2\sin\theta$	Two sides and the included angle **Area of a triangle:** $A = \frac{1}{2}\ a\ b\ sinC$

Trigonometric ratios

For the following **right-angled triangle** we have

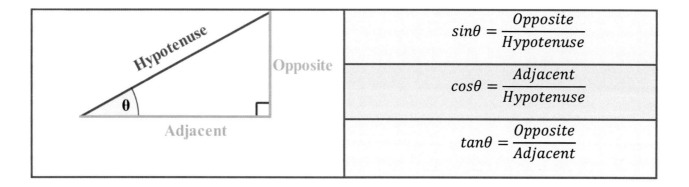

	$sin\theta = \dfrac{Opposite}{Hypotenuse}$
	$cos\theta = \dfrac{Adjacent}{Hypotenuse}$
	$tan\theta = \dfrac{Opposite}{Adjacent}$

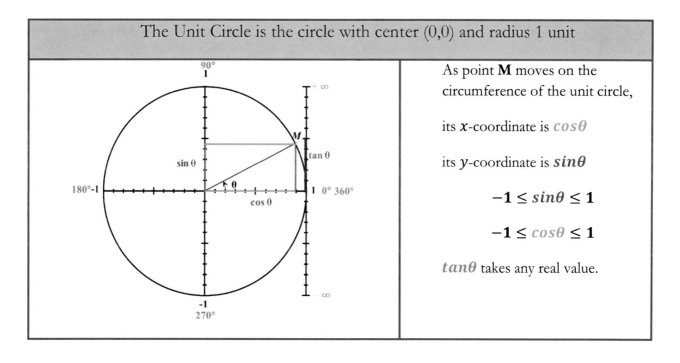

The Unit Circle is the circle with center (0,0) and radius 1 unit

As point **M** moves on the circumference of the unit circle,

its x-coordinate is $cos\theta$

its y-coordinate is $sin\theta$

$$-1 \le sin\theta \le 1$$

$$-1 \le cos\theta \le 1$$

$tan\theta$ takes any real value.

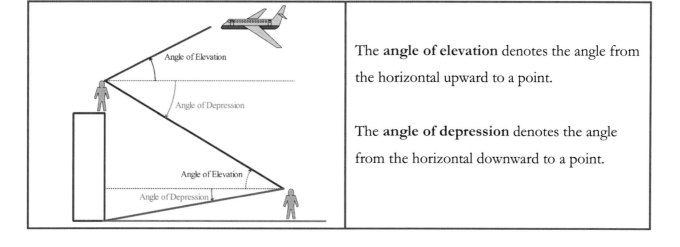

The **angle of elevation** denotes the angle from the horizontal upward to a point.

The **angle of depression** denotes the angle from the horizontal downward to a point.

Trigonometric table of common angles

Degrees	0° or 360°	30°	45°	60°	90°	180°	270°
Radians	0 or 2π	$\frac{\pi}{6}$	$\frac{\pi}{4}$	$\frac{\pi}{3}$	$\frac{\pi}{2}$	π	$\frac{3\pi}{2}$
sin	0	$\frac{1}{2}$	$\frac{\sqrt{2}}{2}$	$\frac{\sqrt{3}}{2}$	1	0	-1
cos	1	$\frac{\sqrt{3}}{2}$	$\frac{\sqrt{2}}{2}$	$\frac{1}{2}$	0	-1	0
tan	0	$\frac{\sqrt{3}}{3}$	1	$\sqrt{3}$	Is not defined	0	Is not defined

Trigonometric table of related angles

	$\frac{\pi}{2}-\theta$	$\frac{\pi}{2}+\theta$	$\pi-\theta$	$\pi+\theta$	$\frac{3\pi}{2}-\theta$	$\frac{3\pi}{2}+\theta$	$-\theta$
sin	$cos\theta$	$cos\theta$*	$sin\theta$	$-sin\theta$	$-cos\theta$	$-cos\theta$	$-sin\theta$
cos	$sin\theta$	$-sin\theta$	$-cos\theta$	$-cos\theta$	$-sin\theta$	$sin\theta$	$cos\theta$

*For example $sin\left(\frac{\pi}{2}+\theta\right)=cos\theta$

Trigonometric Identities

$sin^2\theta+cos^2\theta=1$	$tan\theta=\dfrac{sin\theta}{cos\theta}$
$sin2\theta=2sin\theta cos\theta$	$cos2\theta=cos^2\theta-sin^2\theta=2cos^2\theta-1=1-2sin^2\theta$
$1+tan^2\theta=sec^2\theta\left(=\dfrac{1}{cos^2\theta}\right)$	$1+cot^2\theta=csc^2\theta\left(=\dfrac{1}{sin^2\theta}\right)$

▪ Example of a trigonometric equation

Find the exact solutions of $sin2x=cosx$ for $0\le x\le 2\pi$

$$sin2x=cosx \Rightarrow 2sinx\,cosx=cosx \Rightarrow 2sinx\,cosx-cosx=0 \Rightarrow cosx\,(2sinx-1)=0$$

$cosx=0$ or $2sinx-1=0$

$x=\frac{\pi}{2}$ or $x=\frac{3\pi}{2}$ $sinx=\frac{1}{2}$

$x=\frac{\pi}{6}$ or $x=\frac{5\pi}{6}$

Important: Trigonometric equations can be solved both graphically and analytically (using the general solutions of trigonometric equations or the unit circle) depending on the kind of question and whether this question requires GDC or not.

Example Given that $sinx = \frac{1}{3}$, where $\frac{\pi}{2} \leq x \leq \pi$, evaluate $sin2x$.

Solution

$$sin^2x + cos^2x = 1 \Rightarrow \left(\frac{1}{3}\right)^2 + cos^2x = 1 \Rightarrow cos^2x = 1 - \frac{1}{9}$$

$$\Rightarrow cosx = \pm\sqrt{\frac{8}{9}}, \text{ and since } \frac{\pi}{2} \leq x \leq \pi, \text{ therefore } cosx = -\sqrt{\frac{8}{9}}$$

Therefore, $sin2x = 2sinx\,cosx = 2\,\frac{1}{3}\left(-\sqrt{\frac{8}{9}}\right) = -\frac{4\sqrt{2}}{9}$

- **Sine rule**

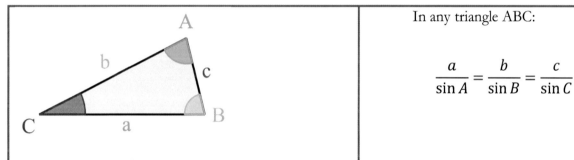

	In any triangle ABC:
	$$\frac{a}{\sin A} = \frac{b}{\sin B} = \frac{c}{\sin C}$$

Ambiguous case: When you are given two adjacent sides of a triangle followed by an angle, the **Sine rule** will give you two answers. The $sin^{-1}x$ function will only give us one of the two angles if we are using a calculator. To find the other one, we need to subtract the calculator's answer from $180°$ or π.

- **Cosine rule**

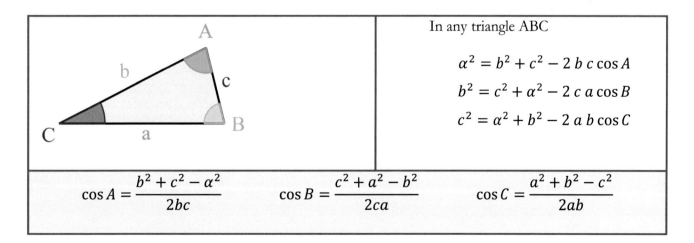

	In any triangle ABC
	$$a^2 = b^2 + c^2 - 2\,b\,c\cos A$$ $$b^2 = c^2 + a^2 - 2\,c\,a\cos B$$ $$c^2 = a^2 + b^2 - 2\,a\,b\cos C$$

$$\cos A = \frac{b^2 + c^2 - a^2}{2bc}$$	$$\cos B = \frac{c^2 + a^2 - b^2}{2ca}$$	$$\cos C = \frac{a^2 + b^2 - c^2}{2ab}$$

Trigonometric Functions

$f(x) = sinx$

Domain: $x \in \mathbb{R}$

Range: $-1 \leq y \leq 1$

Period: 2π

The **Period** is the length that it takes for the curve to start repeating itself.
The **amplitude** of a trigonometric functions $(\sin x, \cos x)$ is the distance between the principal axis and one of the maximum or minimum points.

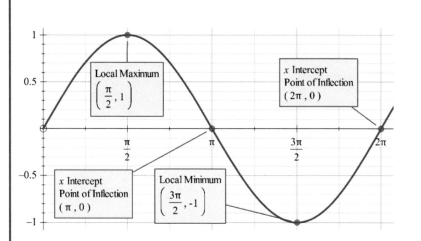

Amplitude: $\frac{y_{max}-y_{min}}{2} = \frac{1-(-1)}{2} = 1$

Principal axis: $y = \frac{y_{max}+y_{min}}{2} = \frac{1+(-1)}{2} = 0$ (the x-axis)

$f(x) = cosx$

Domain: $x \in \mathbb{R}$

Range: $-1 \leq y \leq 1$

Period: 2π

The distance between the x-coordinates of the minimum and maximum of the graphs of $sinx$ or $cosx$ is half of a period.

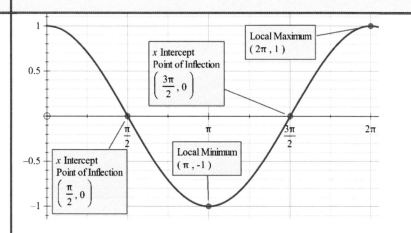

Amplitude: $\frac{y_{max}-y_{min}}{2} = \frac{1-(-1)}{2} = 1$

Principal axis: $y = \frac{y_{max}+y_{min}}{2} = \frac{1+(-1)}{2} = 0$ (the x-axis)

$f(x) = tanx$

Domain: $x \in \mathbb{R} \backslash \left\{ \pm\frac{\pi}{2}, \pm\frac{3\pi}{2}, \pm\frac{5\pi}{2}, .. \right\}$

Range: $y \in \mathbb{R}$

Period: π

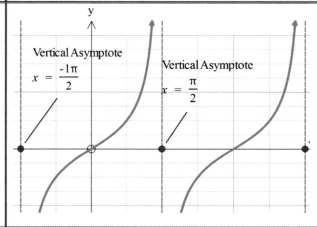

Vertical Asymptotes: $x = \frac{\pi}{2}, x = -\frac{\pi}{2}, x = \frac{3\pi}{2}, ...$

Trigonometric Graph Transformations

$a\,sin[b\,(x-h)]+v$ $a\,cos[b\,(x-h)]+v$	$a\,tan[b\,(x-h)]+v$
Amplitude: $|a|$, Period: $\frac{2\pi}{b}$, h: Horizontal shift v: Vertical shift, principal axis: $y=v$	a: Vertical stretch, Period: $\frac{\pi}{b}$, h: Horizontal shift v: Vertical shift The tangent function does not have an amplitude because it does not have a minimum or maximum value.

Example

Find the period, the amplitude, the principal axis, the horizontal, and the vertical shift of the following trigonometric functions.

(i) $2sin(3x)+3$

(ii) $4cos(2(x-4))-2$

(iii) $-\frac{1}{2}\sin(8(x+2))+5$

(iv) $3\tan(4(x+1))$

Solution

(i)   Period: $\frac{2\pi}{3}$, amplitude: 2, principal axis: $y=3$, vertical shift: 3 units upward.

(ii) Period: $\frac{2\pi}{2}=\pi$, amplitude: 4, principal axis: $y=-2$, horizontal shift: 4 units to the right, vertical shift: 2 units downward.

(iii) Period: $\frac{2\pi}{8}=\frac{\pi}{4}$, amplitude: $\frac{1}{2}$, principal axis: $y=5$, horizontal shift: 2 units to the left.

(iv) Period: $\frac{\pi}{4}$, horizontal shift: 1 unit to the left and a vertical stretch by a scale factor of 3.

Important: Interesting applications of trigonometric functions are the height of tide and the motion of a Ferris wheel.

Note: There are a lot of applications of sine and cosine rules on problems include navigation, three-dimensional shapes, and angles of elevation and depression.

The **bearing** to a point is the angle measured in a **clockwise** direction from the **north**.	

General Solutions of Trigonometric Equations (Optional but very useful)

$$sinx = sin\theta \Leftrightarrow \begin{cases} x = 2\kappa\pi + \theta \\ \quad or \\ x = 2\kappa\pi + (\pi - \theta) \end{cases}, \quad \kappa \in \mathbb{Z}$$

$$cosx = cos\theta \Leftrightarrow \begin{cases} x = 2\kappa\pi + \theta \\ \quad or \\ x = 2\kappa\pi - \theta \end{cases}, \quad \kappa \in \mathbb{Z}$$

$$tanx = tan\theta \Leftrightarrow x = \kappa\pi + \theta, \quad \kappa \in \mathbb{Z}$$

$$cotx = cot\theta \Leftrightarrow x = \kappa\pi + \theta, \quad \kappa \in \mathbb{Z}$$

Example Find the exact solutions of $sin2x = \frac{1}{2}$ for $0 \leq x \leq 2\pi$.

Solution

$$sin2x = \frac{1}{2} \Rightarrow sin2x = sin\frac{\pi}{6} \Rightarrow \begin{cases} 2x = 2\kappa\pi + \frac{\pi}{6} \\ \quad or \\ 2x = 2\kappa\pi + (\pi - \frac{\pi}{6}) \end{cases}$$

$$\Rightarrow \begin{cases} x = \kappa\pi + \frac{\pi}{12} \\ \quad or \\ x = \kappa\pi + \frac{5\pi}{12} \end{cases} \overset{0 \leq x \leq 2\pi}{\Longrightarrow} x = \frac{\pi}{12}, \frac{5\pi}{12}, \pi + \frac{\pi}{12}, \pi + \frac{5\pi}{12} \Rightarrow x = \frac{\pi}{12}, \frac{5\pi}{12}, \frac{13\pi}{12}, \frac{17\pi}{12}$$

Compound angle trigonometric identities	Double angle trigonometric identities
$sin(\alpha \pm b) = sin\alpha cosb \pm cos\alpha sinb$	$sin2\alpha = 2sin\alpha cos\alpha$
$cos(\alpha \pm b) = cos\alpha cosb \mp sin\alpha sinb$	$cos2\alpha = cos^2\alpha - sin^2\alpha = 2cos^2\alpha - 1$ $= 1 - 2sin^2\alpha$
$tan(\alpha \pm b) = \dfrac{tan\alpha \pm tanb}{1 \mp tan\alpha tanb}$	$tan2\alpha = \dfrac{2tan\alpha}{1 - tan^2\alpha}$
$cot(\alpha \pm b) = \dfrac{cot\alpha cotb \mp 1}{cotb \pm cot\alpha}$	$cot2\alpha = \dfrac{cot^2\alpha - 1}{2cot\alpha}$

Reciprocal Trigonometric Functions

Cosecant

$$f(x) = cosecx = \frac{1}{sinx}$$

$$D_f: x \in \mathbb{R}, x \neq k\pi, k \in \mathbb{Z}$$

$$R_f: y \leq -1 \text{ or } y \geq 1$$

Vertical asymptotes:

$$x = k\pi, k \in \mathbb{Z}$$

Period: 2π

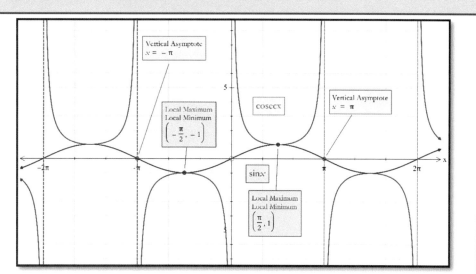

Secant

$$f(x) = secx = \frac{1}{cosx}$$

$$D_f: x \in \mathbb{R},$$

$$x \neq \frac{(2k+1)\pi}{2}, k \in \mathbb{Z}$$

$$R_f: y \leq -1 \text{ or } y \geq 1$$

Vertical asymptotes:

$$x = \frac{(2k+1)\pi}{2}, k \in \mathbb{Z}$$

Period: 2π

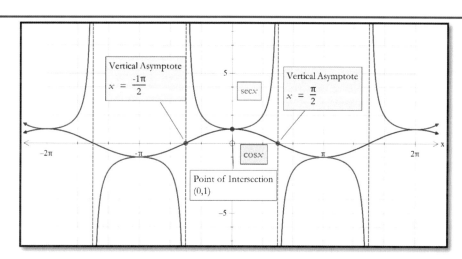

Cotangent

$$f(x) = cotx = \frac{1}{tanx}$$

$$D_f: x \in \mathbb{R},$$
$$x \neq k\pi, k \in \mathbb{Z}$$
$$R_f = \mathbb{R}$$

Vertical asymptotes:
$$x = k\pi, k \in \mathbb{Z}$$

Period: π

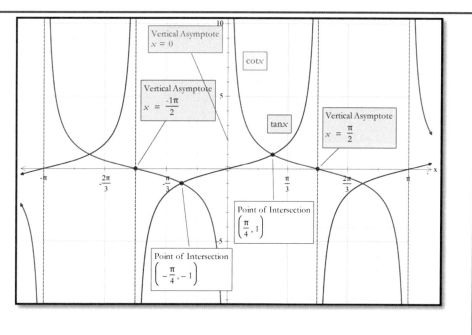

Inverse Trigonometric Functions

$$f(x) = arcsinx = sin^{-1}x$$

$$D_f = [-1,1]$$

$$R_f = \left[-\frac{\pi}{2}, \frac{\pi}{2}\right]$$

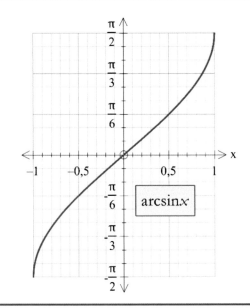

$$f(x) = arccosx = cos^{-1}x$$

$$D_f = [-1,1]$$

$$R_f = [0, \pi]$$

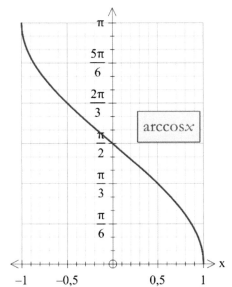

$$f(x) = arctanx = tan^{-1}x$$

$$D_f = \mathbb{R}$$

$$R_f = \left(-\frac{\pi}{2}, \frac{\pi}{2}\right)$$

Horizontal asymptotes:

$$y = -\frac{\pi}{2}, y = \frac{\pi}{2}$$

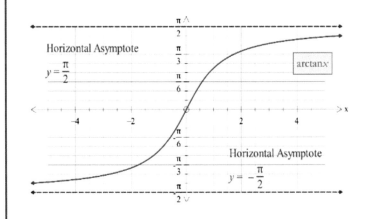

Continuity - Differentiation

Definition A function $f(x)$ is **continuous** at $x = a$ if $f(a)$ is defined and

$$\lim_{x \to a} f(x) = f(a)$$

This definition implies that the function f has the following three properties if f is continuous at $x = a$:

(i) a is in the domain of f.

(ii) $\lim\limits_{x \to a} f(x)$ exists , i.e. $\lim\limits_{x \to a^-} f(x) = \lim\limits_{x \to a^+} f(x)$.

(iii) $\lim\limits_{x \to a} f(x) = f(a)$.

Definition A function f is **continuous** on an interval, if it is continuous at every number in the interval.

Note: Less formally, a function is continuous when its graph is a single unbroken curve i.e., we could draw the graph without lifting our pen from the paper.

▨   The following types of functions are continuous at every point in their domains:

Polynomials, Rational functions, Exponential functions, Logarithmic functions, and trigonometric functions.

▨   If f and g are **continuous** at a and c is constant, then so are

$f + g, f \cdot g, f \circ g, cf, \dfrac{f}{g}$ where $g(x) \neq 0$.

Definition If a function f is **not continuous** at a point c, we say that f is **discontinuous** at c and call c a point of **discontinuity** of f.

Types of discontinuities		
Point discontinuity	Infinite discontinuity	Jump discontinuity
$\lim\limits_{x \to c} f(x) \neq f(c)$ or $f(c)$ does not exist	$\lim\limits_{x \to c} f(x) = +\infty \, or -\infty$	$\lim\limits_{x \to c^-} f(x) \neq \lim\limits_{x \to c^+} f(x)$

Derivative

The **tangent line** to the curve $y = f(x)$ at the point $A(x, f(x))$ is the line through A with slope (gradient)

$$f'(x) = \lim_{h \to 0} \left(\frac{f(x+h) - f(x)}{h} \right)$$

which is called the **derivative** of $f(x)$ at x.

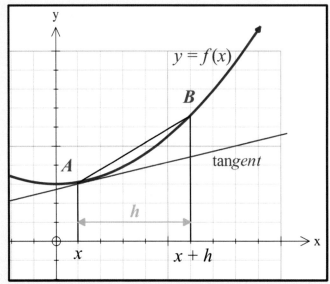

The **rate of change** of the function f at $A(x, f(x))$ is given by the gradient of the tangent to the curve at A.

Apart from the **Newtonian**[1] notation (placing a dash $f'(x)$) there is also the **Leibniz**[2] notation $\left(\frac{dy}{dx} \right)$ for the derivative of the function $y = f(x)$

$$f'(x) = y' = \frac{dy}{dx} = \frac{df}{dx} = \frac{d}{dx} f(x)$$

$\frac{dy}{dx}$ measures the **rate of change** of y in respect of x.

Higher Derivatives

$$f'(x) = \frac{dy}{dx}, f''(x) = \frac{d^2 y}{dx^2}, f'''(x) = \frac{d^3 y}{dx^3}, \dots, f^{(n)}(x) = \frac{d^n y}{dx^n}$$

[1]{Sir Isaac Newton (1643-1727)}, [2]{Gottfried Wilhelm Leibniz (1646-1716)}

Example

Find, from first principles, the derivative of $f(x) = x^2$.

Solution

At any point x the derivative is given by

$$f'(x) = \lim_{h \to 0} \frac{f(x+h) - f(x)}{h} = \lim_{h \to 0} \frac{(x+h)^2 - x^2}{h} =$$

$$= \lim_{h \to 0} \frac{x^2 + 2xh + h^2 - x^2}{h} = \lim_{h \to 0} \frac{(2x+h)h}{h} = \lim_{h \to 0} (2x+h) = 2x$$

Thus, the derivative (or gradient) function is $f'(x) = 2x$.

Differentiation Rules

- $\left(f(x) \pm g(x) \right)' = f'(x) \pm g'(x)$

- $\left(cf(x) \right)' = cf'(x)$

- $\left(f(x) \times g(x) \right)' = f'(x) \times g(x) + f(x) \times g'(x)$ Product rule (Newtonian notation)

- $y = uv \Rightarrow \dfrac{dy}{dx} = u\dfrac{dv}{dx} + v\dfrac{du}{dx}$ Product rule (Leibniz notation)

- $\left(\dfrac{f(x)}{g(x)} \right)' = \dfrac{f'(x) \cdot g(x) - f(x) \cdot g'(x)}{(g(x))^2}$ Quotient rule (Newtonian notation)

- $y = \dfrac{u}{v} \Rightarrow \dfrac{dy}{dx} = \dfrac{v\frac{du}{dx} - u\frac{dv}{dx}}{v^2}$ Quotient rule (Leibniz notation)

- $(f \circ g)'(x) = f'\left(g(x) \right) \times g'(x)$ Chain rule (Newtonian notation)

- $y = g(u), u = f(x) \Rightarrow \dfrac{dy}{dx} = \dfrac{dy}{du} \times \dfrac{du}{dx}$ Chain rule (Leibniz notation)

Theorem: If f is differentiable at x_0, then f is continuous at x_0.

Hence, **differentiability** implies **continuity**.

Note: It is possible for a function to be continuous at $x = x_0$ and not be differentiable at $x = x_0$. For example, the function $f(x) = |x|$ is continuous at $x = 0$ but it is not differentiable at $x = 0$.

An important trigonometric limit is the following:

$$\lim_{\theta \to 0} \frac{\sin\theta}{\theta} = 1$$

Example

Find $\lim\limits_{\theta \to 0} \dfrac{\tan 4\theta}{5\theta}$

Solution

$$\lim_{\theta \to 0} \frac{\tan 4\theta}{5\theta} = \lim_{\theta \to 0} \frac{\sin 4\theta}{5\theta \cos 4\theta} = \lim_{\theta \to 0} \frac{\sin 4\theta}{4\theta} \frac{4}{5\cos 4\theta} = 1 \cdot \frac{4}{5} = \frac{4}{5}$$

Since, as $\theta \to 0$ then $4\theta \to 0$

$$\lim_{4\theta \to 0} \frac{\sin 4\theta}{4\theta} = 1$$

and $\lim\limits_{\theta \to 0} \cos 4\theta = 1$

Example (Continuity)

The function f is defined by $f(x) = \begin{cases} 3x + 4, & x \le 1 \\ ax^3 - bx - 2, & x > 1 \end{cases}$ where $a, b \in \mathbb{R}$

Given that f and its derivative f' are continuous in the domain of f, find the values of a and b.

Solution

Since f is continuous, this implies that $\lim\limits_{x \to 1^-} f(x) = \lim\limits_{x \to 1^+} f(x) = f(1) \Rightarrow 7 = a - b - 2 = 7 \Rightarrow$

$$a - b = 9$$

$$f'(x) = \begin{cases} 3, & x \le 1 \\ 3ax^2 - b, & x > 1 \end{cases}$$

Since f' is continuous, this implies that

$$\lim_{x \to 1^-} f'(x) = \lim_{x \to 1^+} f'(x) = f'(1) \Rightarrow 3 = 3a - b = 3 \Rightarrow 3a - b = 3$$

Therefore, $\begin{cases} a - b = 9 \\ 3a - b = 3 \end{cases} \Rightarrow a = -3, b = -12.$

Function	Derivative
$f(x) = c$	$f'(x) = 0$
$f(x) = x$	$f'(x) = 1$
$f(x) = x^k, \quad k \in \mathbb{R}$	$f'(x) = kx^{k-1}, \quad k \in \mathbb{R}$
$f(x) = sinx$	$f'(x) = cosx$
$f(x) = cosx$	$f'(x) = -sinx$
$f(x) = tanx$	$f'(x) = sec^2x$
$f(x) = secx$	$f'(x) = secx\ tanx$
$f(x) = cscx$	$f'(x) = -cscx\ cotx$
$f(x) = cotx$	$f'(x) = -csc^2x$
$f(x) = arcsinx$	$f'(x) = \dfrac{1}{\sqrt{1-x^2}}$
$f(x) = arccosx$	$f'(x) = -\dfrac{1}{\sqrt{1-x^2}}$
$f(x) = arctanx$	$f'(x) = \dfrac{1}{1+x^2}$
$f(x) = e^x$	$f'(x) = e^x$
$f(x) = a^x$	$f'(x) = a^x lna$
$f(x) = lnx\ , x > 0$	$f'(x) = \dfrac{1}{x}, x > 0$
$f(x) = \log_a x\ , x > 0$	$f'(x) = \dfrac{1}{xlna}, x > 0$
Composite Function	Derivative
$f(x) = [g(x)]^k$	$f'(x) = k[g(x)]^{k-1}g'(x)$
$f(x) = sin(g(x))$	$f'(x) = cos(g(x)) \times g'(x)$
$f(x) = cos(g(x))$	$f'(x) = -sin(g(x)) \times g'(x)$
$f(x) = e^{g(x)}$	$f'(x) = e^{g(x)} \times g'(x)$
$f(x) = \ln[g(x)]\ , g(x) > 0$	$f'(x) = \dfrac{g'(x)}{g(x)}$

Examples

1. Find the derivative of $f(x) = \dfrac{x^2 e^x + sin^3 x}{lnx}$

Solution (Newtonian notation)

$$f'(x) = \left(\frac{x^2 e^x + sin^3 x}{lnx}\right)' = \frac{(x^2 e^x + sin^3 x)' lnx - (x^2 e^x + sin^3 x)(lnx)'}{(lnx)^2} =$$

$$= \frac{[(x^2 e^x)' + (sin^3 x)'] lnx - (x^2 e^x + sin^3 x)\frac{1}{x}}{(lnx)^2} =$$

$$= \frac{2xe^x lnx + x^2 e^x lnx + 3sin^2 x\, cosx\, lnx - (x^2 e^x + sin^3 x)\frac{1}{x}}{(lnx)^2}$$

2. Find the derivative of $y = (4x - 12)^6$

Solution (Leibniz notation)

Let $u = 4x - 12$ and $y = u^6$

Thus, $\dfrac{dy}{du} = 6u^5$ and $\dfrac{du}{dx} = 4$

Since $\dfrac{dy}{dx} = \dfrac{dy}{du}\dfrac{du}{dx} \Rightarrow \dfrac{dy}{dx} = 6u^5 \cdot 4 = 24u^5 = 24(4x - 12)^5$

Equations of Tangent and Normal

The equation of the **tangent** to a curve $y = f(x)$ at (x_1, y_1) is given by

$$y - y_1 = f'(x_1)(x - x_1)$$

Since the slope (m_T) of the tangent is $m_T = f'(x_1)$.

The equation of the **normal** (the perpendicular to the tangent) to a curve $y = f(x)$ at (x_1, y_1) is given by

$$y - y_1 = -\frac{1}{f'(x_1)}(x - x_1)$$

Since the slope (m_N) of the normal is $m_N = -\dfrac{1}{m_T} = -\dfrac{1}{f'(x_1)}$

Note: When the first derivative (the slope of the tangent) at a certain point (x_1, y_1) is equal to zero ($f'(x_1) = 0$) then the equation of the tangent at this point is given by the equation: $y = y_1$ (a horizontal line) and the equation of the normal at this point is a vertical line of the form $x = x_1$. A **vertical tangent** touches the curve at a point where the gradient of the curve is infinite and undefined.

Example
Find the equations of the tangent and the normal to the curve $y = x^3$ at the point $(2,8)$.
Solution
$$f'(x) = 3x^2 \Rightarrow f'(2) = 3 \times 2^2 = 12$$
So, the slope of the tangent is $m_T = 12$, the slope of the normal is $m_N = -\frac{1}{12}$
and the corresponding equations are given by the following formulas:
The equation of the **tangent** at $(2,8): y - 8 = 12(x - 2)$
The equation of the **normal** at $(2,8): y - 8 = -\frac{1}{12}(x - 2)$

Implicit differentiation

Many equations may be written explicitly where the variable y is explicitly written as a function of x.

For example, $y = 3x^3 + 5x + 4$.

However, in many cases, it is difficult or even impossible to solve an equation in x and y to obtain y explicitly in terms of x and then try to differentiate. In this case, we would use implicit differentiation. Implicit differentiation allows an expression to be differentiated even when y cannot be expressed explicitly in terms of x. For example, $x^2 y^5 + \cot(xy^2) = 4x$.

The process of implicit differentiation may be described as follows:

1.   Differentiate both sides of the equation with respect to x using the differentiation rules and mainly the chain rule.

2.   Collect the terms $\frac{dy}{dx}$ on one side of the equation and solve for $\frac{dy}{dx}$.

Each time we take the derivative of a term containing y, we must multiply its derivative by $\frac{dy}{dx}$. When we differentiate terms involving y, we must use the chain rule because y is an implied differentiable function of x.

▪   With implicit differentiation, we can find the slope $\frac{dy}{dx}$, for curves which are not necessarily functions.

Example

Given the curve $\cos(x^2y) = \sin(y^2)$, find $\frac{dy}{dx}$.

Solution

$$\frac{d}{dx}(\cos(x^2y)) = \frac{d}{dx}(\sin(y^2)) \Rightarrow -\sin(x^2y)\frac{d}{dx}(x^2y) = \cos(y^2)\frac{d}{dx}(y^2) \Rightarrow$$

$$\Rightarrow -\sin(x^2y)\left(y\frac{d}{dx}x^2 + x^2\frac{dy}{dx}\right) = \cos(y^2)2y\frac{dy}{dx} \Rightarrow$$

$$\Rightarrow -2xy\sin(x^2y) - x^2\frac{dy}{dx}\sin(x^2y) = 2y\cos(y^2)\frac{dy}{dx} \Rightarrow$$

$$\Rightarrow -2xy\sin(x^2y) = 2y\cos(y^2)\frac{dy}{dx} + x^2\frac{dy}{dx}\sin(x^2y) \Rightarrow$$

$$\Rightarrow -2xy\sin(x^2y) = \frac{dy}{dx}\left(2y\cos(y^2) + x^2\sin(x^2y)\right) \Rightarrow$$

$$\Rightarrow \frac{dy}{dx} = \frac{-2xy\sin(x^2y)}{2y\cos(y^2) + x^2\sin(x^2y)}$$

Related rates of change

A related rate problem is a problem that often occurs in physical applications where the several related variables are changing with an independent variable (usually time). The rates of change of the variable quantities must also be related.

The steps involved in solving such a problem may be described as follows:

1. Draw a diagram and label the quantities that vary if possible.
2. Find an equation that relates the various variable quantities of the problem.
3. Differentiate both sides of the previous equation with respect to an independent variable (usually the independent variable will be time), using the chain rule and implicit differentiation when needed.
4. Use the information provided in the resulting equation and solve for the unknown rate of change.

Example: An ice cube is melting at a rate $1\ cm^3/sec$. How fast is its surface area changing when the side is $0.5\ cm$?

Solution

The volume (V) and the surface area (A) of the cube are given by the following formulas:

$V(x) = x^3$ and $A(x) = 6x^2$. We want to find $\frac{dA}{dt}$ when $\frac{dV}{dt} = -1$ and $x = 0.5$.

The volume (V) is decreasing at a rate of $1\ cm^3/sec$, so $\frac{dV}{dt} = -1$.

If we differentiate implicitly both expressions, we have

$$\frac{dV}{dt} = \frac{d}{dt}(x^3) = 3x^2\frac{dx}{dt} \Rightarrow -1 = 3x^2\frac{dx}{dt} \Rightarrow \frac{dx}{dt} = -\frac{1}{3x^2}$$

$$\frac{dA}{dt} = \frac{d}{dt}(6x^2) = 12x\frac{dx}{dt} = 12x \times \frac{-1}{3x^2} = -\frac{1}{4x}$$

Now we can use the given numerical value $x = 0.5$:

$$\frac{dA}{dt} = -\frac{1}{4 \times 0.5} = -\frac{1}{2}cm^2/sec$$

Thus, the surface area is decreasing at a rate of $-0.5\ cm^2/sec$.

Stationary points

A **stationary point** is a point where $f'(x) = 0$. It could be a local **minimum**, local **maximum** or a **stationary point of inflection.**

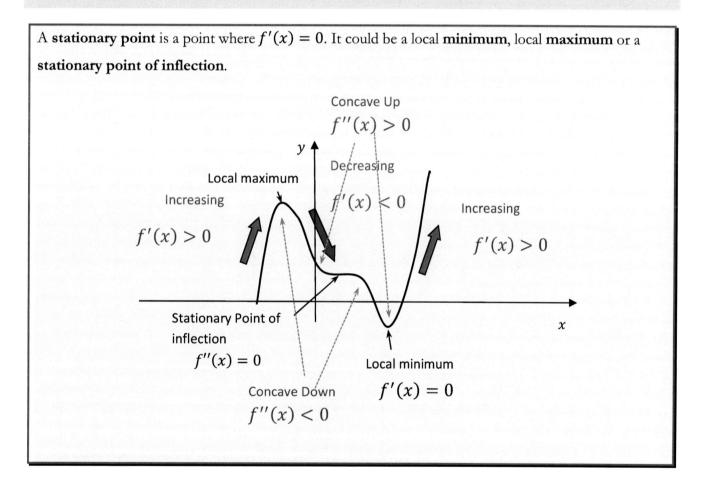

Points of inflection (inflexion)

A **point of inflection** is a point on a curve at which a change of **concavity** occurs.

We have a point of inflection at $x = x_0$ if $f''(x_0) = 0$ **and** the sign of $f''(x)$ changes on either side of $x = x_0$.

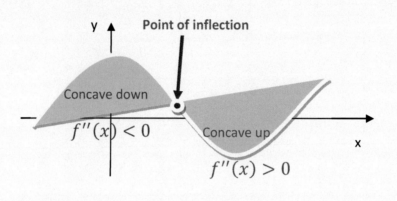

Test for increasing/decreasing

- If $f'(x) > 0$ on an interval, then f is increasing on this interval.

- If $f'(x) < 0$ on an interval, then f is decreasing on this interval.

Test for concavity (concave-up / concave-down)

- f is concave-up on an interval I if $f''(x) > 0$ for all x on I.

- f is concave-down on an interval I if $f''(x) < 0$ for all x on I.

The First Derivative Test for turning points (maximum/minimum)

Suppose x_0 is a stationary point $(f'(x_0) = 0)$ of a continuous function f.

- If f' changes from positive to negative at x_0, then f has a **local maximum** at x_0.

		x_0	
f'	+	0	-
f	↗	max	↘

■ If f' changes from negative to positive at x_0, then f has a **local minimum** at x_0.

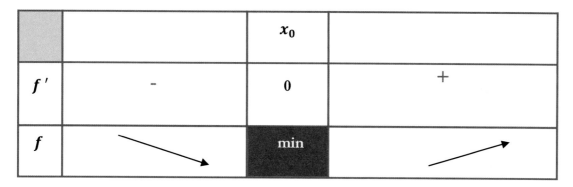

		x_0	
f'	-	0	+
f	↘	min	↗

The Second Derivative Test for turning points (maximum/minimum)

■ If $f'(x_0) = 0$ and $f''(x_0) > 0$, then f has a local minimum at x_0.

■ If $f'(x_0) = 0$ and $f''(x_0) < 0$, then f has a local maximum at x_0.

Note: If we have a closed interval, apart from the stationary points we should also examine the endpoints for maximum or minimum. This is a common thing when we try to find a minimum or a maximum in an **optimization problem.**

The graph of the derivative function $f'(x)$

The following guidelines are useful in order to sketch the derivative function $f'(x)$ given the graph of the original function $f(x)$ and vice versa:

1. If the graph of $f(x)$ is **increasing** then $f'(x)$ is **positive** and vice versa.
2. If the graph of $f(x)$ is **decreasing** then $f'(x)$ is **negative** and vice versa.
3. If the graph of $f(x)$ is **concave-up** then the graph of $f'(x)$ is **increasing** and vice versa.
4. If the graph of $f(x)$ is **concave-down** then the graph of $f'(x)$ is **decreasing** and vice versa.
5. If the graph of $f(x)$ has a **stationary point** then the graph of $f'(x)$ has a **zero** and vice versa.
6. If the graph of $f(x)$ has a **point of inflection** then the graph of $f'(x)$ has **a turning point** and vice versa.

Example

We can obtain the graph of $f'(x)$ from the graph of $f(x)$ by applying the rules above

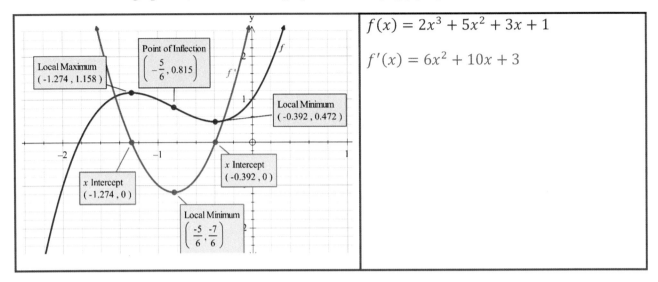

$$f(x) = 2x^3 + 5x^2 + 3x + 1$$

$$f'(x) = 6x^2 + 10x + 3$$

Optimization Problems

Many application problems in calculus involve functions for which you want to find maximum or minimum values. First, we have to write down the "constraint" equation and the "optimization" equation. Then, we have to express the optimization equation as a function of only one variable, and, if it is needed, reduce it to be easily differentiable. Finally, we have to differentiate the function and set it equals zero in order to find the stationary points. If we have a closed interval, apart from the stationary points, we should also examine the endpoints for maximum or minimum. This is a common thing when we try to find a minimum or a maximum in an optimization problem.

Example

A closed cylindrical tin is to be made from a sheet of metal measuring $600\pi \ cm^2$. Find the dimensions of the tin if the volume is to be maximum.

Solution

The total surface area of a closed cylinder is

$$A = 2\pi r^2 + 2\pi rh = 600\pi$$

$$h = \frac{600\pi - 2\pi r^2}{2\pi r} = \frac{600 - 2r^2}{2r} = \frac{300 - r^2}{r}$$

and the volume is $V = \pi r^2 h = \pi r^2 \frac{300 - r^2}{r} = 300\pi r - \pi r^3$

$$V'(r) = (300\pi r - \pi r^3)' = 300\pi - 3\pi r^2 = 0$$

$$r = \sqrt{\frac{300}{3}} = \sqrt{100} = 10$$

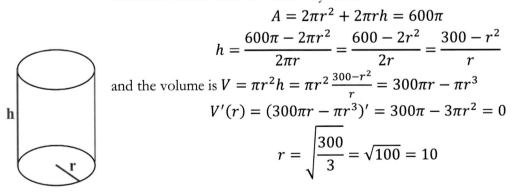

Since $V'(r) > 0$ when $r < 10$ and $V'(r) < 0$ when $r > 10$, we can conclude that the volume is maximized when $r = 10 \, cm$ and $h = \frac{600-2\times10^2}{2\times10} = \frac{600-200}{20} = 20$ cm.

Curve sketching of $y = f(x)$

- Identify the **domain** of f, that is, the set of values of x for which f is defined.
- Find f' and f''.
- Find x -axis intercepts setting $y = 0$ and solve for x.
- Find y -axis intercept setting $x = 0$ and solve for y.
- Find **Horizontal** (behavior of f as $x \to \pm\infty$) and **Vertical Asymptotes** (where the function is not defined).
- Find where the curve is **increasing** $(f'(x) > 0)$ and where it is **decreasing** $(f'(x) < 0)$.
- Find where the curve is **concave up** $(f''(x) > 0)$ and where it is **concave down** $(f''(x) < 0)$.
- Find **Local Minimum, Maximum** values and **points of inflection**.
- Find any **Symmetry** (<u>even function</u>: $f(-x) = f(x)$, which indicates symmetry about the y-axis, <u>odd function</u>: $f(-x) = -f(x)$, which indicates symmetry about the origin) the curve may have.

Example

Sketch the graph of $f(x) = \frac{x}{x^2-1}$

Solution

- The domain is $\{x \in \mathbb{R}, x \neq -1,1\}$.
- The x-axis and y-axis intercept is the origin $(0,0)$.
- $f'(x) = \frac{(x)'(x^2-1)-x(x^2-1)'}{(x^2-1)^2} = \frac{(x^2-1)-2x^2}{(x^2-1)^2} = -\frac{x^2+1}{(x^2-1)^2} < 0$
- $f''(x) = \left(-\frac{x^2+1}{(x^2-1)^2}\right)' = \cdots = \frac{2x(x^2+3)}{(x^2-1)^3}$

	$-\infty$	-1	0	1	$+\infty$
$f''(x)$		-	+	-	+
$f'(x)$		-	-	-	-
$f(x)$		Decreasing and **Concave down**	Decreasing and **Concave up**	Decreasing and **Concave down**	Decreasing and **Concave up**

- The function has vertical asymptotes at $x = 1$ and $x = -1$ and a horizontal asymptote at $y = 0$.

- There is no local minimum or maximum, however we have an inflection point at $(0,0)$.

- The function is odd since $f(-x) = \frac{-x}{(-x)^2 - 1} = -f(x)$ which means that the graph is symmetric with respect to the origin.

Finally the graph of $f(x) = \frac{x}{x^2 - 1}$ is the following:

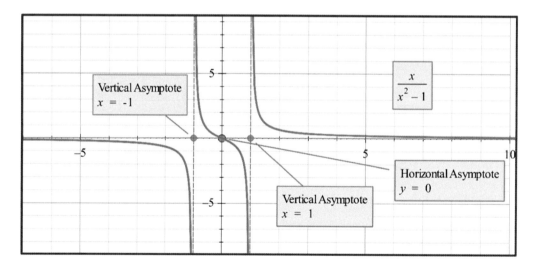

Integration

Indefinite Integral

If $F(x)$ is a function where $F'(x) = f(x)$ then the antiderivative of $f(x)$ (integrand) is $F(x)$ and the indefinite integral is defined as

$$\int f(x)dx = F(x) + c$$

Definite Integral

A definite integral is of the form

$$\int_{a}^{b} f(x)dx$$

where x is called the variable of integration and $\boldsymbol{a}, \boldsymbol{b}$ are called the **Lower** and **Upper limit** respectively.

$$\int_{a}^{b} f(x)d\,x = F(b) - F(a) = [F(x)]_{a}^{b}$$

where $F(x)$ is the antiderivative of $f(x)$.

Properties of Indefinite Integrals

- $\int f'(x)dx = f(x) + c$

- $(\int f(x)dx)' = f(x)$

- $\int kf(x)dx = k \int f(x)dx$, where k is a constant.

- $\int (f(x) \pm g(x))dx = \int f(x)dx \pm \int g(x)dx$

Properties of Definite Integrals

- $\int_a^a f(x)dx = 0$

- $\int_a^b f(x)dx = -\int_b^a f(x)dx$

- $\int_a^b (-f(x))dx = -\int_a^b f(x)dx$

- $\int_a^b kf(x)dx = k\int_a^b f(x)dx$, where k is a constant.

- $\int_a^b f(x)dx + \int_b^c f(x)dx = \int_a^c f(x)dx$

- $\int_a^b ((f(x) \pm g(x))dx = \int_a^b f(x)dx \pm \int_a^b g(x)dx$

Basic Indefinite Integrals

$\int k\,dx = kx + c$	$\int a^x dx = \dfrac{a^x}{\ln a} + c$
$\int x^n dx = \dfrac{x^{n+1}}{n+1} + c$ $(n \neq -1)$	$\int (ax+b)^n dx = \dfrac{1}{a}\dfrac{(ax+b)^{n+1}}{n+1} + c$ $(n \neq -1)$
$\int \dfrac{1}{x}dx = \ln|x| + c$	$\int \dfrac{1}{ax+b}dx = \dfrac{1}{a}\ln|ax+b| + c$
$\int e^x dx = e^x + c$	$\int e^{ax+b}dx = \dfrac{1}{a}e^{ax+b} + c$
$\int \sin x\,dx = -\cos x + c$	$\int \sin(ax+b)\,dx = -\dfrac{1}{a}\cos(ax+b) + c$
$\int \cos x\,dx = \sin x + c$	$\int \cos(ax+b)\,dx = \dfrac{1}{a}\sin(ax+b) + c$
$\int \dfrac{1}{a^2+x^2}dx = \dfrac{1}{a}\arctan\left(\dfrac{x}{a}\right) + c$	$\int \dfrac{1}{\sqrt{a^2-x^2}}dx = \arcsin\left(\dfrac{x}{a}\right) + c, |x| < a$

Integration Techniques

Integration by Substitution for indefinite integrals

$$\int f(g(x))g'(x)\,dx = \int f(u)du$$

where $u = g(x)$ and $du = g'(x)dx$

Example

Using the substitution $u = x^2 + 5$ find $\int x(x^2+5)^4\,dx$

Solution

If $u = x^2 + 5$ then $\frac{du}{dx} = 2x \implies du = 2xdx$

Therefore, $\int x(x^2+5)^4\,dx = \frac{1}{2}\int (x^2+5)^4\,2xdx = \frac{1}{2}\int u^4\,du = \frac{1}{2}\frac{u^5}{5} + c = \frac{(x^2+5)^5}{10} + c$

Integration by Substitution for definite integrals

$$\int_a^b f(g(x))g'(x)\,dx = \int_{g(a)}^{g(b)} f(u)du$$

where $u = g(x)$ and $du = g'(x)dx$

Example

Using the substitution $u = x^4 + 2018$ find

$$\int_4^5 \frac{x^3}{x^4 + 2018}\,dx$$

Solution

If $u = x^4 + 2018$ then $\frac{du}{dx} = 4x^3 \implies du = 4x^3dx$

To find the new limits of integration we note that

when $x = 4$, $u = 4^4 + 2018 = 256 + 2018 = 2274$

and when $x = 5$, $u = 5^4 + 2018 = 625 + 2018 = 2643$

Thus,

$$\int_4^5 \frac{x^3}{x^4+2018}dx = \frac{1}{4}\int_4^5 \frac{4x^3}{x^4+2018}dx = \frac{1}{4}\int_{2274}^{2643}\frac{1}{u}du = \frac{1}{4}[\ln|u|]_{2274}^{2643} =$$

$$= \frac{1}{4}(\ln 2643 - \ln 2274)$$

Trigonometric Substitution

Expression	Substitution
$\sqrt{a^2-x^2}$	$x = a\sin\theta, \quad \theta \in \left[-\frac{\pi}{2},\frac{\pi}{2}\right]$
$\sqrt{a^2+x^2}$	$x = a\tan\theta, \quad \theta \in \left(-\frac{\pi}{2},\frac{\pi}{2}\right)$
$\sqrt{x^2-a^2}$	$x = a\sec\theta, \quad \theta \in \left[0,\frac{\pi}{2}\right) \cup \left[\pi,\frac{3\pi}{2}\right)$

Example

Find $\int \sqrt{1-x^2}\,dx$.

Solution

If $x = \sin\theta$, $\theta \in \left[-\frac{\pi}{2},\frac{\pi}{2}\right]$ then $\frac{dx}{d\theta} = \cos\theta \Rightarrow dx = \cos\theta d\theta$

Therefore $\int \sqrt{1-x^2}\,dx = \int \sqrt{1-\sin^2\theta}\cos\theta d\theta = \int \sqrt{\cos^2\theta}\cos\theta d\theta =$

$$= \int \cos^2\theta d\theta = \frac{1}{2}\int (1+\cos2\theta)d\theta = \frac{1}{2}\int d\theta + \frac{1}{2}\int \cos2\theta\,d\theta =$$

$$= \frac{1}{2}\theta + \frac{1}{4}\sin2\theta + c = \frac{1}{2}\theta + \frac{1}{2}\sin\theta\cos\theta + c$$

If $x = \sin\theta$ then $\theta = \arcsin x$ and the previous expression becomes

$$\frac{1}{2}\arcsin x + \frac{1}{2}x\sqrt{1-\sin^2\theta} + c = \frac{1}{2}\arcsin x + \frac{1}{2}x\sqrt{1-x^2} + c$$

Integration by Parts

$$\int u \frac{dv}{dx} dx = uv - \int v \frac{du}{dx} dx$$

Integration by parts is used to evaluate integrals when the usual integration techniques cannot be applied. Our objective in using integration by parts is to obtain a simpler integral than the one we started with. In general, when deciding on a choice for u, we usually try to choose u to be a function that becomes simpler when differentiated. A useful rule (that usually works) is setting u with the following priority:

1. $\ln f(x)$ (Logarithm)
2. $arcsin(f(x)), arcos(f(x)), arctan(f(x))$ (Inverse trigonometric function)
3. Power of x
4. $e^{f(x)}$, $sinf(x)$, $cosf(x)$

Repeated integration by parts

In some cases, applying the integration by parts formula, one time may not be enough. You may need to apply it more than one time.

For example, the integral $\int x^2 e^x dx$ can be found applying integration by parts twice. Similarly the integral $\int x^3 sinx dx$ can be found using integration by parts three times.

Examples

1. Find $\int x\, e^x dx$

Solution

Applying the integration by parts formula with $u = x$ and $\frac{dv}{dx} = e^x$

so that $\frac{du}{dx} = 1$ and $v = e^x$

Then, $\int x\, e^x dx = xe^x - \int e^x dx = xe^x - e^x + c$

2. Find $\int x \, lnx \, dx$

Solution

Applying the integration by parts formula with $u = lnx$ and $\frac{du}{dx} = \frac{1}{x}$, $\frac{dv}{dx} = x$ and $v = \frac{1}{2}x^2$

gives $\int x \, lnx \, dx = \frac{1}{2}x^2 lnx - \int \frac{1}{2}x^2 \frac{1}{x} dx = \frac{1}{2}x^2 lnx - \frac{1}{2}\int x dx = \frac{1}{2}x^2 lnx - \frac{1}{4}x^2 + c$

3. Find $\int lnx \, dx$

Solution

Applying the integration by parts formula with $u = lnx$ and $\frac{du}{dx} = \frac{1}{x}$, $\frac{dv}{dx} = 1$ and

$v = x$ gives $\int lnx \, dx = xlnx - \int x\frac{1}{x}dx = xlnx - \int dx = xlnx - x + c = x(lnx - 1) + c$

4. Find $I = \int e^x \, sinxdx$

Solution

Applying the integration by parts formula with $u = e^x$ and $\frac{dv}{dx} = sinx$

so that $\frac{du}{dx} = e^x$ and $v = -cosx$

Then, $I = \int e^x \, sinxdx = -e^x cosx - \int e^x (-cosx)dx = -e^x cosx + \int e^x \, cosxdx$

We now integrate by parts one more time with $u = e^x$ and $\frac{dv}{dx} = cosx$

so that $\frac{du}{dx} = e^x$ and $v = sinx$

Then, $\int e^x \, cosxdx = e^x sinx - \overbrace{\int e^x \, sinxdx}^{I}$

We observe that we have ended up with exactly the same integral as the one we started with.

Therefore, $I = -e^x cosx + \int e^x \, cosxdx = -e^x cosx + e^x sinx - I \Rightarrow$

$$2I = -e^x cosx + e^x sinx \Rightarrow I = \int e^x \, sinxdx = \frac{e^x(sinx - cosx)}{2} + c$$

Trigonometric Integrals

Odd powers of Sine and Cosine using the trigonometric identity:

$$cos^2x + sin^2x = 1$$

Example

Find $\int sin^3x \, dx$

Solution

$$\int sin^3x \, dx = \int sinx \; sin^2x \, dx = \int sinx(1 - cos^2x) \, dx =$$

$$= \int (sinx - sinxcos^2x) \, dx = \int sinx \, dx - \int sinx \; cos^2x \, dx = -cosx + \frac{cos^3x}{3} + c$$

Even powers of Sine and Cosine using the trigonometric identities:

$$cos^2x = \frac{1}{2}(1 + cos2x) \; or \; sin^2x = \frac{1}{2}(1 - cos2x)$$

Example

Find $\int sin^4x \, dx$

Solution

$$\int sin^4x \, dx = \int (sin^2x)^2 \, dx = \int [\frac{1}{2}(1 - cos2x)]^2 \, dx =$$

$$= \int \frac{1}{4}(1 - 2cos2x + cos^2 2x)dx = \int \frac{1}{4}dx - \frac{1}{2}\int cos2x \, dx + \frac{1}{4}\int cos^2 2x \, dx =$$

$$= \frac{1}{4}x - \frac{sin2x}{4} + \frac{1}{4}\int \frac{1}{2}(1 + cos4x) \, dx = \frac{1}{4}x - \frac{sin2x}{4} + \frac{1}{8}x + \frac{sin4x}{32} + c =$$

$$= \frac{3}{8}x - \frac{sin2x}{4} + \frac{sin4x}{32} + c$$

Powers of Tangent using the trigonometric identity:

$$tan^2x + 1 = sec^2x$$

Example

Find $\int tan^4x\, dx$

Solution

$$\int tan^4x\, dx = \int tan^2x\, tan^2x\, dx = \int tan^2x(sec^2x - 1)\, dx =$$

$$= \int tan^2x\, sec^2x\, dx - \int tan^2x\, dx = \frac{tan^3x}{3} - \int (sec^2x - 1)\, dx =$$

$$= \frac{tan^3x}{3} - \int sec^2x\, dx + \int dx = \frac{tan^3x}{3} - tanx + x + c$$

Splitting the numerator

In order to evaluate an integral with a fractional expression, it is sometimes helpful to split the numerator to produce a simpler integral.

Examples

$\int \frac{x+4}{x+10}\, dx = \int \frac{x+(10-6)}{x+10}\, dx = \int \frac{x+10}{x+10}\, dx - \int \frac{6}{x+10}\, dx = x - 6\ln|x+10| + c$

$\int \frac{x}{3x+10}\, dx = \frac{1}{3}\int \frac{3x}{3x+10}\, dx = \frac{1}{3}\int \frac{3x+10-10}{3x+10}\, dx = \frac{1}{3}\int \frac{3x+10}{3x+10}\, dx - \frac{1}{3}\int \frac{10}{3x+10}\, dx =$

$$= \frac{1}{3}\int dx - \frac{1}{3}\int \frac{10}{3x+10}\, dx = \frac{1}{3}\, x - \frac{10}{9}\ln|3x+10| + c$$

Long division

In case of an integral of a rational function of the form $\int \frac{P(x)}{Q(x)} dx$ where the degree of polynomial $P(x)$ is greater than or equal to the degree of polynomial $Q(x)$, we use the long division in order to produce a simpler integral.

Example

Find $\int \frac{x^3+4}{x+1} dx$

Solution

The division statement is $\frac{x^3+4}{x+1} = (x^2 - x + 1) + \frac{3}{x+1}$

This enables us to write:

$$\int \frac{x^3 + 4}{x + 1} dx = \int \left(x^2 - x + 1 + \frac{3}{x + 1} \right) dx = \frac{1}{3}x^3 - \frac{1}{2}x^2 + x + 3ln|x + 1| + c$$

Integration using partial fractions

The integral of rational functions of the form $\frac{P(x)}{Q(x)}$, where the degree of polynomial $P(x)$ is less than the degree of polynomial $Q(x)$, can be obtained by splitting the integrand into simpler rational expressions (partial fractions). Many integrals involving rational expressions can be found if we first do partial fractions on the integrand.

Example

Find $\int \frac{x+5}{(x-4)(x-1)} dx$

Solution

$$\frac{x + 5}{(x - 4)(x - 1)} = \frac{A}{(x - 4)} + \frac{B}{(x - 1)} = \frac{A(x - 1) + B(x - 4)}{(x - 4)(x - 1)} \Rightarrow$$

$$\Rightarrow x + 5 = A(x - 1) + B(x - 4) \Rightarrow x + 5 = (A + B)x + (-A - 4B) \Rightarrow$$

$$\Rightarrow \begin{cases} A + B = 1 \\ -A - 4B = 5 \end{cases} \Rightarrow \begin{cases} A = 3 \\ B = -2 \end{cases}$$

Thus, $\int \frac{x+5}{(x-4)(x-1)} dx = \int \left(\frac{3}{(x-4)} - \frac{2}{(x-1)} \right) dx = 3ln|x - 4| - 2ln|x - 1| + c$

Completing the square to use a trigonometric substitution

By completing the square we are able to convert an integral that includes a quadratic expression into a form that allow us to use a trigonometric substitution. The general completing the square formula is:

$$x^2 + ax + b = x^2 + ax + \left(\frac{a}{2}\right)^2 - \left(\frac{a}{2}\right)^2 + b = \left(x + \frac{a}{2}\right)^2 + b - \frac{a^2}{4}$$

Example

Find $\int \frac{1}{x^2+4x+13} dx$

Solution

$$\int \frac{1}{x^2 + 4x + 13} dx = \int \frac{1}{(x + 2)^2 + 13 - 4} dx = \int \frac{1}{(x + 2)^2 + 3^2} dx =$$

$$= \frac{1}{3} arctan\left(\frac{x + 2}{3}\right) + c$$

Note: The value of some definite integrals can only be found using GDC.

Applications of Integration

Areas above and below the x-axis

For a function $f(x) \geq 0$ on an interval $[a, b]$, the area between the x-axis and the curve $y = f(x)$ between $x = a$ and $x = b$, is given by

$$A_1 = \int_a^b f(x)dx$$

For a function $f(x) \leq 0$ on an interval $[b, c]$, the area between the x-axis and the curve $y = f(x)$ between $x = b$ and $x = c$, is given by

$$A_2 = -\int_b^c f(x)dx$$

Finally, the total area between the curve and the x-axis on the interval $[a, c]$ is given by

$$A = A_1 + A_2$$

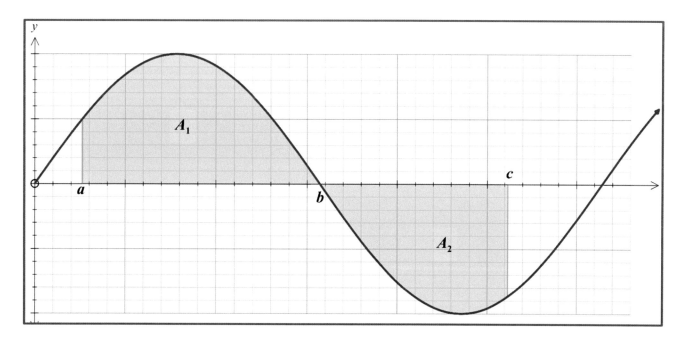

Example

Find the area of the region enclosed by the curve $f(x) = x(x-1)(x-2)$ and the x-axis.

Solution

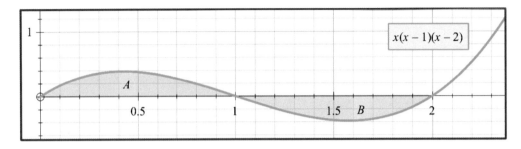

The curve crosses the x-axis at $x = 0$, $x = 1$ and $x = 2$.

The function is positive on the interval $[0,1]$ and negative on $[1,2]$.

Therefore the required area is

$$A + B = \int_0^1 x(x-1)(x-2)\, dx + \left|\int_1^2 x(x-1)(x-2)\, dx\right| =$$

$$= \int_0^1 (x^3 - 3x^2 + 2x)dx - \int_1^2 (x^3 - 3x^2 + 2x)dx =$$

$$= \left[\frac{1}{4}x^4 - x^3 + x^2\right]_0^1 - \left[\frac{1}{4}x^4 - x^3 + x^2\right]_1^2 =$$

$$= \frac{1}{4} - 1 + 1 - \left(4 - 8 + 4 - \frac{1}{4} + 1 - 1\right) = \frac{1}{2} \text{ square units}$$

The area between a curve and the y-axis

The area between a curve and the y-axis, between $y = a$ and $y = b$, is given by

$$A = \int_a^b x\, dy$$

Example

Find the area of the region enclosed by the curve $y = \sqrt{x - 1}$, the y-axis, the lines $y = 1$ and $y = 2$.

Solution

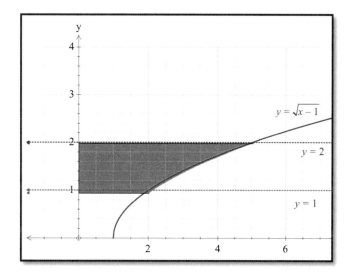

In order to find the area, we should express x in terms of y

$$y = \sqrt{x - 1} \Longrightarrow y^2 = x - 1 \Longrightarrow x = y^2 + 1$$

and then we have to calculate the following integral

$$A = \int_1^2 (y^2 + 1)dy = \left[\frac{1}{3}y^3 + y\right]_1^2 = \frac{8}{3} + 2 - \frac{1}{3} - 1 = \frac{10}{3} \text{ square units.}$$

The area between two curves

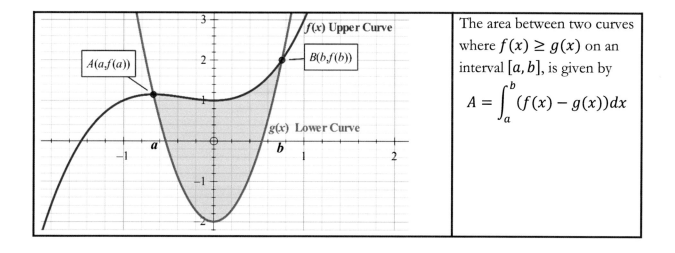

The area between two curves where $f(x) \geq g(x)$ on an interval $[a, b]$, is given by

$$A = \int_a^b (f(x) - g(x))dx$$

Example

Find the area of the region enclosed by the curves $f(x) = x^2$ and $g(x) = x^3$.

Solution

To find the coordinates of the common points solve together $x^2 = x^3 \Rightarrow$

$$\Rightarrow x^3 - x^2 = 0 \Rightarrow x^2(x-1) = 0 \Rightarrow x = 0 \ or \ x = 1$$

Solving the inequality $x^2 \geq x^3$ or sketching the graph on GDC, we observe that $f(x) \geq g(x)$ on the interval $[0,1]$.

Therefore the shaded area is given by

$$A = \int_0^1 (x^2 - x^3)dx = \left[\frac{1}{3}x^3 - \frac{1}{4}x^4\right]_0^1 = \frac{1}{3} - \frac{1}{4} = \frac{1}{12} \text{ square units}$$

Volumes of revolution

When a plane region bounded by the curve $y = f(x)$ and the vertical lines $x = a$ and $x = b$ is revolved about the x-axis, the volume of revolution is given by

$$V_x = \pi \int_a^b y^2 dx$$

When a plane region enclosed by the curves $y = f(x)$ (upper curve) and $y = g(x)$ (lower curve), and the vertical lines $x = a$ and $x = b$ is revolved about the x-axis, the volume of revolution, is given by

$$V_x = \pi \int_a^b ([f(x)]^2 - [g(x)]^2)dx$$

When a plane region bounded by the curve $y = f(x)$ and the horizontal lines $y = a$ and $y = b$ is revolved about the y-axis, the volume of revolution is given by

$$V_y = \pi \int_a^b x^2 dy$$

Example

Find the volume of the solid generated when the line $y = 2x$ for $0 \leq x \leq 2$ is revolved around the x-axis.

Solution

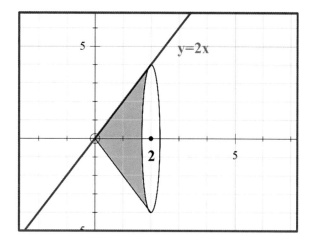

The volume of the revolution around the x- axis is given by

$$V_x = \pi \int_0^2 y^2 dx = \pi \int_0^2 4x^2 dx = \pi \left[\frac{4}{3}x^3 \right]_0^2 = \frac{32\pi}{3}$$

Example

Find the volume of the solid generated when the line $y = 2x^3$ for $0 \leq y \leq 16$ is revolved around the y-axis.

Solution

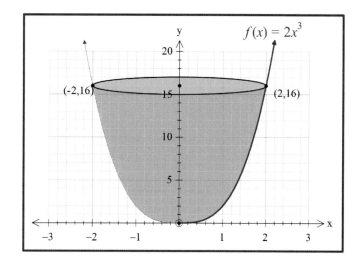

$$y = 2x^3 \Rightarrow x^3 = \frac{y}{2} \Rightarrow x = \left(\frac{y}{2}\right)^{1/3}$$

The volume of the revolution around the x- axis is given by

$$V_y = \pi \int_0^2 x^2 dy = \pi \int_0^2 \left(\left(\frac{y}{2}\right)^{1/3}\right)^2 dy = \frac{\pi}{\sqrt[3]{4}} \int_0^2 y^{\frac{2}{3}} dy = \frac{\pi}{\sqrt[3]{4}} \left[\frac{3}{5} y^{\frac{5}{3}}\right]_0^2 =$$

$$\frac{\pi}{\sqrt[3]{4}} \times \frac{3}{5} \times 2^{\frac{5}{3}} = \frac{3 \times 2 \times \sqrt[3]{4}\pi}{5\sqrt[3]{4}} = \frac{6}{5}\pi$$

Example

Find the **exact** value of the volume of the solid generated when the function $f(x) = x^3 + lnx$ for $1 \le y \le e^3 + 1$ is rotated through 2π about the y- axis.

Solution

The volume of the revolution around the y- axis is given by the following formula:

$$V_y = \pi \int_a^b x^2 dy = \pi \int_1^{e^3+1} x^2 dy$$

We observe that it is very difficult (even impossible) to find the inverse of the function f, so instead, we can apply the following technique:

$$y = x^3 + lnx \Rightarrow \frac{dy}{dx} = 3x^2 + \frac{1}{x} \Rightarrow dy = \left(3x^2 + \frac{1}{x}\right) dx$$

When $y = 1$ then $1 = x^3 + lnx \Rightarrow x = 1$

and if $y = e^3 + 1$ then $e^3 + 1 = x^3 + lnx \Rightarrow x = e$

So, the integral $\pi \int_1^{e^3+1} x^2 dy$ can be written in respect to x as follows:

$$\pi \int_1^e x^2 \left(3x^2 + \frac{1}{x}\right) dx = \pi \int_1^e (3x^4 + x) dx = \pi \left[\frac{3x^5}{5} + \frac{x^2}{2}\right]_1^e =$$

$$= \pi \left(\frac{3e^5}{5} + \frac{e^2}{2} - \frac{3 \times 1^5}{5} - \frac{1^2}{2}\right) = \pi \left(\frac{6e^5 + 5e^2 - 11}{10}\right)$$

Kinematics

Let a particle P moves in a straight line, and its displacement (position) is $s(t)$ relative to a point O at a given time t.

	If $s(t) = 0$ then P is at O.
	If $s(t) > 0$ then P is to the right of O.
	If $s(t) < 0$ then P is to the left of O.
	If $v(t) = 0$ then P is at rest.
	If $v(t) > 0$ then P is moving to the right.
	If $v(t) < 0$ then P is moving to the left.

If $a(t) = 0$ then the velocity may be a minimum or maximum or constant.

If $a(t) > 0$ then the velocity is increasing.

If $a(t) < 0$ then the velocity is decreasing.

The **velocity** $v(t)$ of the particle P at time t is the rate of change of the displacement.

$$v(t) = \frac{ds}{dt}$$

The **acceleration** $a(t)$ of the particle P at time t is the rate of change of the velocity or the second derivative of the displacement.

$$a(t) = \frac{dv}{dt} = \frac{d^2s}{dt^2} = v\frac{dv}{ds}$$

The **speed** of the particle P at time t is the absolute value of the velocity at this time.

$$\text{Speed} = |v(t)|$$

Important: If the signs of $v(t)$ and $a(t)$ are both positive or both negative (they have the same sign) then the speed of the particle is increasing. If the signs of $v(t)$ and $a(t)$ are opposite, then the speed of the particle is decreasing.

The **velocity** $v(t)$ of the particle P is the integral of the acceleration.

$$v(t) = \int a(t)dt$$

The **displacement** $s(t)$ of the particle P is the integral of the velocity.

$$s(t) = \int v(t)dt$$

The **total distance** (d) travelled from t_1 to t_2 is given by the following definite integral:

$$d = \int_{t_1}^{t_2} |v(t)|dt$$

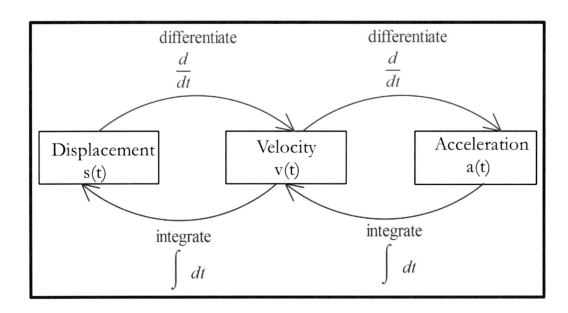

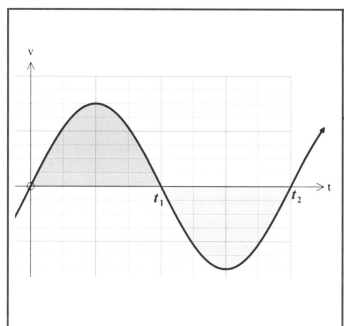

The **displacement** over the interval $[0, t_2]$ is given by

$$s = \int_0^{t_2} v(t)dt$$

The **distance** covered over the interval $[0, t_2]$ is given by

$$d = \int_0^{t_1} v(t)dt - \int_{t_1}^{t_2} v(t)dt$$

$$= \int_0^{t_2} |v(t)|dt$$

Example

The velocity v of a particle at time t is given by $v(t) = t^3 + 2t^2 + 10t + 4$ and when $t = 4\ sec$, the displacement $s = 14\ m$. Find an equation of the displacement at any time t.

Solution

$$s = \int (t^3 + 2t^2 + 10t + 4)dt = \frac{1}{4}t^4 + \frac{2}{3}t^3 + \frac{10}{2}t^2 + 4t + c$$

When $t = 4$ then $s = 14$

$$\frac{1}{4}4^4 + \frac{2}{3}4^3 + \frac{10}{2}4^2 + 4 \cdot 4 + c = 14 \Rightarrow c = -\frac{566}{3}$$

Therefore the displacement is given by $s(t) = \frac{1}{4}t^4 + \frac{2}{3}t^3 + \frac{10}{2}t^2 + 4t - \frac{566}{3}$

Statistics

Population: The entire group you want to know something about.

Sample: The group you use to infer something about the population.

Random Sample is a set of n objects in a population of N objects where all possible samples are equally likely to happen.

Continuous data is data that can be assigned an infinite number of values between whole numbers. (A person's height or weight)

Discrete data is data that can be counted. (Number of students)

Bar chart is a graph that uses vertical or horizontal bars to represent the frequencies of the categories in a data set. (Categorical variables)

Histogram is a graphical display of a frequency or a relative frequency distribution that uses classes and vertical bars of various heights to represent the frequencies (Quantitative variables).

A frequency polygon is a graph that displays the data using lines to connect points plotted for the frequencies. The frequencies represent the heights of the vertical bars in the histograms.

A stem and leaf plot is a table where all the data must be first sorted in ascending order, and then each data value is split into a "stem" (the first digit or digits) and a "leaf" (usually the last digit).

Measures of Central Tendency

Mean of a set of values is the number obtained by adding the values and dividing the total by the number of values. In the formula below x_i represents an observation of the data, f_i the corresponding frequency and n the total number of observations.

The population mean is usually denoted by μ and the sample mean is denoted by $\bar{x}$ (read as 'x-bar').

$$\mu \overset{*}{=} \bar{x} = \frac{1}{n}\sum_{i=1}^{k} f_i x_i$$	$$n = \sum_{i=1}^{k} f_i$$

* In IB exams data will be treated as the population.

Notes:

- Calculation of mean can be performed by using either the formula or technology.
- When the data are grouped into classes, we should use the midpoint or mid-interval value to represent all values within that interval in order to estimate the mean of grouped data.

Example

Find the mean of a sample of 6 test grades $(80, 65, 91, 75, 82, 76)$

Answer

$$\bar{x} = \frac{\sum_{i=1}^{6} x_i}{6} = \frac{80 + 65 + 91 + 75 + 82 + 76}{6} \cong 78.17$$

Example (Grouped Data)

Estimate the mean and write down the modal class of the following heights

Heights (cm)	158-160	161-163	164-166	167-169	170-172	173-175	176-178	179-181
Mid-height x_i (cm)	159	162	165	168	171	174	177	180
Frequency f_i	2	4	4	5	7	6	3	1

From the table above, we have that

$$\sum_{i=1}^{8} f_i = 2 + 4 + 4 + 5 + 7 + 6 + 3 + 1 = 32$$

and

$$\sum_{i=1}^{8} f_i x_i = 159 \times 2 + 162 \times 4 + 165 \times 4 + 168 \times 5 + 171 \times 7 + 174 \times 6 + 177 \times 3 + 180 \times 1$$
$$= 5418$$

$$\bar{x} = \frac{\sum f_i x_i}{\sum f_i} = \frac{5418}{32} = 169.31$$

The **modal class** is $170 - 172$ since it has the largest frequency (7).

- The **Median** of a data set is the middle value when the data values are arranged in ascending or descending order. If the data set has an even number of entries, the median is the mean of the two middle data entries.

Examples

1. Sample $(8,3,5,12,15,20,1), n = 7$

Answer

Step 1: arrange in ascending order $1,3,5,\mathbf{8},12,15,20$

Step 2: the median is $\mathbf{8}$

2. Sample $(8,3,5,12,15,20,1,13), n=8$

Answer

Step 1: arrange in ascending order $1,3,5,\mathbf{8},\mathbf{12},13,15,20$

Step 2: the median (m) is given by $m = \frac{8+12}{2} = \mathbf{10}$

- The **mode** of a data set is the value that occurs most frequently. When two values occur with the same greatest frequency, each one is a mode, and the data set is bimodal. When more than two values occur with the same greatest frequency, each is a mode and data set is said to be multimodal. When no value is repeated, we say there is no mode.

Example

Find the mode of a sample of 7 test grades (80, 65, 91, 75, 82, 76, 82).

Answer

The **mode** is grade 82 because it has the greatest frequency (=2).

- In a **negatively skewed distribution**, the mean is to the left of the median, and the mode is to the right of the median.

$$\textbf{Mean} < \textbf{Median} < \textbf{Mode}$$

- In a **symmetrical distribution**, the data values are evenly distributed on both sides of the mean. Also, when the distribution is unimodal, the mean, median, and mode are all equal and are located at the center of the distribution.

$$\textbf{Mean} = \textbf{Median}$$

- In a **positively skewed distribution**, the mean is to the right of the median, and the mode is to the left of the median.

$$\textbf{Mode} < \textbf{Median} < \textbf{Mean}$$

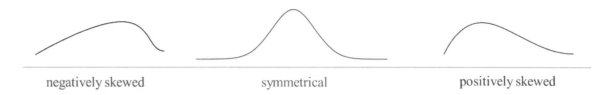

negatively skewed   symmetrical   positively skewed

Measures of Dispersion

Range=largest measurement-smallest measurement

Example

Sample ($12, 15, 18, 20, 17$)

    Range=max-min=20-12=8

Variance	Standard Deviation
$\sigma^2 \overset{*}{=} s_n^2 = \dfrac{1}{n}\displaystyle\sum_{i=1}^{n} f_i(x_i - \mu)^2 = \dfrac{1}{n}\displaystyle\sum_{i=1}^{n} f_i x_i{}^2 - \mu^2$	$s_n = \sqrt{\dfrac{1}{n}\displaystyle\sum_{i=1}^{n}(x_i - \bar{x})^2}$

* In IB exams data will be treated as the population.

Notes:

- Standard deviation is the square root of the variance.
- Calculation of standard deviation and variance can be also performed using GDC.

Percentiles

Let $0 < p < 100$. The pth percentile is a number x such that $p\%$ of all measurements fall below the pth percentile and $(100 - p)\%$ fall above it.

Lower Quartile (25th percentile)	Median (50th percentile)	Upper Quartile (75th percentile)
Q_1	Q_2	Q_3

The Interquartile range (IQR) of a data set is the difference between the third and first quartile.

$$IQR = Q_3 - Q_1$$

Box-and-whisker plot

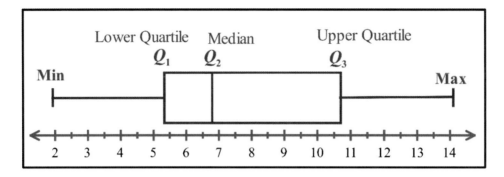

▨ The ends of the box are the **upper** (Q_3) and **lower** (Q_1) quartiles, so the box spans the **interquartile range**(IQR)

$$IQR = Q_3 - Q_1$$

▨ The **median** (Q_2) is marked by a vertical line inside the box.
▨ The **whiskers** are the two lines outside the box that extend to the maximum and minimum observations.
▨ An **outlier** is a point which falls more than 1.5 times the interquartile range $(1.5 \times IQR)$ above the third quartile or below the first quartile.

Important: A GDC may be used to produce **histograms** and **box-and-whisker plots**.

- If we **add** or **subtract** a positive constant value c to/from all the numbers in the dataset, the **mean** (and the **median**) will also **increase** or **decrease**, respectively, by c and the **standard deviation** (and the **variance**) **will** remain the **same**.
- If we **multiply** or **divide** all the numbers in the dataset by a positive constant value c, the **mean**, the **median** and the **standard deviation** will be **multiplied** or **divided**, respectively, by c. It follows that the **variance** will be **multiplied** or **divided** by c^2.

Example

A data set has a mean of 24 and a standard deviation of 4.

(a) Each value in the data set has 7 added to it. Find the new mean, the new standard deviation, and the new variance.
(b) Each value in the data set is multiplied by 5. Find the new mean, the new standard deviation, and the new variance.

Answer

(a) The new mean is $24 + 7 = 31$, and both the standard deviation and variance remain the same.

(b) The new mean is $24 \times 5 = 120$, the new standard deviation is $4 \times 5 = 20$, and the new variance is $20^2 = 400$.

Example of a cumulative frequency diagram

The following cumulative frequency table displays the marks obtained in a test by a group of 80 students. The cumulative frequency is calculated by accumulating the frequencies as we move down the table.

Grades	Frequency	Cumulative frequency
[0-20]	5	5
(20-40]	10	15
(40-60]	25	40
(60-80]	25	65
(80-100]	15	80

The corresponding cumulative frequency diagram is presented below:

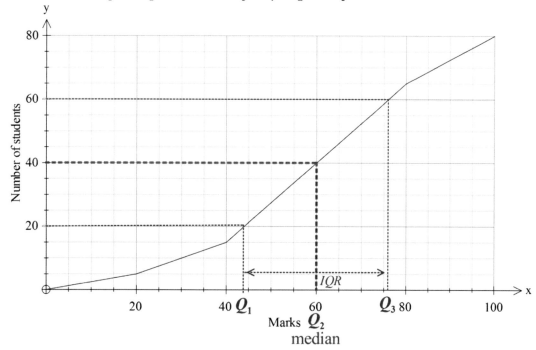

The **median** is estimated using the 50th percentile. As 50% of 80 is 40, we draw a horizontal line parallel to x-axis (Marks), passing through 40 until this line cuts the curve. Then we draw a vertical line parallel to y-axis (Number of students) until it reaches the x-axis, in this case, the value is 60 marks. Similarly, the lower and upper quartiles Q_1, Q_3 can be found at a cumulative frequency of 20 (25th percentile) and 60 (75th percentile) number of students respectively. Following the above steps, we get $Q_1 = 44$ and $Q_3 = 76$. Thus, the interquartile range is $IQR = Q_3 - Q_1$.

Probability & Combinatorics

- A **sample space** U (Universal Set) is the set of all possible outcomes of an experiment.
- An **event** is one or more outcomes of an experiment. Mathematically, an event is a subset of a sample space. For example, scoring a four on the throw of a die.
- An **event** is **simple** if it consists of just a single outcome, and is **compound** otherwise.
- A sample space is discrete if it consists of a finite or countable infinite set of outcomes. A sample space is continuous if it contains an interval (either finite or infinite) of real numbers.
- The set containing no elements is called an **empty set** (or null set) and denote it by $\emptyset$.

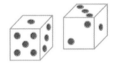

Example

If we toss a coin three times and record the result, the sample space is

$$U = \{HHH, HHT, HTH, HTT, THH, THT, TTH, TTT\}$$

where (for example) THH means 'Tails on the first toss, then heads, then heads again'.

The **theoretical probability** of an occurring event A is given by

$$P(A) = \frac{N(A)}{N(U)} = \frac{Number\ of\ outcomes\ in\ which\ A\ occurs}{Total\ number\ of\ outcomes\ in\ the\ sample\ space\ U}$$

Axioms of probability

1. $0 \leq P(A) \leq 1$

2. $P(\emptyset) = 0$ and $P(U) = 1$

3. If A and B are both subsets of U and they are **mutually exclusive** ($A \cap B = \emptyset$), then

$$P(A \cup B) = P(A) + P(B)$$

We also have the following propositions:

- $P(A') = 1 - P(A)$, where A' is the complement event of A.

- If $A \subseteq B$ then $P(A) \leq P(B)$.

- $P(A \cup B) = P(A) + P(B) - P(A \cap B)$.

Example

A six-sided die is rolled twice. What is the probability that the sum of the numbers is at least 10?

Answer

The number of elements in the sample space is $6^2 = 36$. To obtain a sum of 10 or more, the possibilities for the numbers are $(4,6), (5,5), (6,4), (5,6), (6,5)$ or $(6,6)$. So the probability of the event "that the sum of the numbers is at least 10" is $\dfrac{6}{36} = \dfrac{1}{6}$.

Example

A box contains 4 red and 5 blue disks. A disk is randomly selected and has its color noted. The disk is not replaced and a second disk is then selected.

(a) Find the probability that the disks will be of a different color.
(b) Find the probability that they will be both red.

Answer

The tree diagram for this information is:

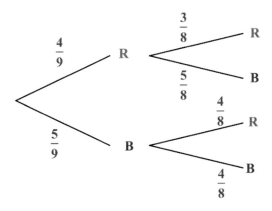

(a) $P(different\ color) = P(RB) + P(BR) = \dfrac{4}{9} \times \dfrac{5}{8} + \dfrac{5}{9} \times \dfrac{4}{8} = \dfrac{40}{72}$

(b) $P(both\ red) = P(RR) = \dfrac{4}{9} \times \dfrac{3}{8} = \dfrac{12}{72}$

Venn Diagrams {John Venn (1834 –1923)}

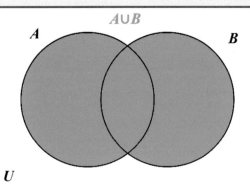

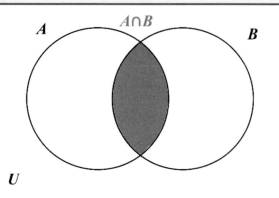

The **Union** of A and B is the set whose elements are all the elements of A and B. $$A \cup B = \{x : x \in A \text{ or } x \in B\}$$ $$P(A \cup B) = P(A) + P(B) - P(A \cap B)$$	The **Intersection** of A and B is the set consisting of the elements that belong to both A and B. $$A \cap B = \{x : x \in A \text{ and } x \in B\}$$

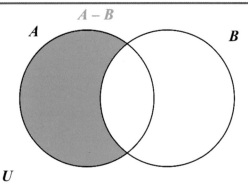

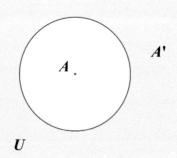

The **Difference** of A and B is the set consisting of those elements of A that are not in B. $$A - B = \{x : x \in A \text{ and } x \notin B\}$$ $$P(A - B) = P(A) - P(A \cap B)$$	The **Complement** of A is the set consisting of those elements of U that are not in A. $$A' = A^c = U - A = \{x \in U : x \notin A\}$$ $$P(A') = 1 - P(A)$$

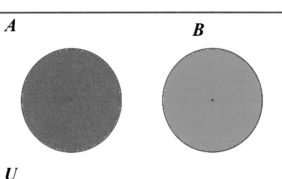	If $A \cap B = \emptyset$ the events A and B are said to be **disjoint** or **mutually exclusive**. Disjoint sets are sets which do not have elements in common. $$P(A \cup B) = P(A) + P(B)$$

Conditional Probability

The probability of an event given that another event has already occurred is a conditional probability.

If A and B are two events, then the **conditional probability** of event A **given (/)** an event B can be found by the formula

$$P(A/B) = \frac{P(A \cap B)}{P(B)}, P(B) \neq 0$$

It should also be noted that usually $P(A/B) \neq P(B/A)$

Bayes' theorem   {Thomas Bayes (1701–1761)}

$$P(B/A) = \frac{P(B)P(A/B)}{P(B)P(A/B) + P(B')P(A/B')}$$

Example

A lot of 1000 semiconductor chips contains 40 that are defective. Two are selected randomly, without replacement, from the lot.

(a) What is the probability that the first one selected is defective?

(b) What is the probability that the second one selected is defective **given** that the first one was defective?

(c) What is the probability that both are defective?

Solution

Let A: The first one selected is defective

and B: The second one selected is defective

Then:

(a) $P(A) = \frac{40}{1000} = 0.04$

(b) $P(B/A) = \frac{P(B \cap A)}{P(A)} = \frac{\frac{40}{1000} \cdot \frac{39}{999}}{\frac{40}{1000}} = \frac{39}{999}$

(c) $P(B \cap A) = \frac{40}{1000} \cdot \frac{39}{999} = \frac{156}{99900}$

Independence

Two events A and B are said to be **independent** if

$$P(A \cap B) = P(A) \times P(B)$$

alternatively, $P(A/B) = P(A)$ and $P(B/A) = P(B)$

Properties of independence

- If A and B are independent then A and B' are independent.
- If A and B are independent, so are A' and B'.

Note: A common mistake is to confuse whether two events are **independent** or **mutually exclusive**. A and B are mutually exclusive events or disjoint if $P(A \cap B) = 0$, that is, the occurrence of one precludes that of the other.

Examples

1. If $P(A/B) = 0.5$, $P(B) = 0.7$ and $P(A) = 0.4$, are the events A and B independent?

Answer The events are not independent because $P(A/B) \neq P(A)$

2. Given that, $P(A) = 0.7, P(B) = 0.5$ and that A and B are **independent** events. Find the probability of the following events: **(a)** $A \cap B$ **(b)** $A \cup B$ **(c)** A/B' **(d)** $A' \cap B$

Solution The events are independent, therefore

(a) $P(A \cap B) = P(A) \times P(B) = 0.7 \times 0.5 = 0.35$

(b) $P(A \cup B) = P(A) + P(B) - P(A \cap B) = 0.7 + 0.5 - 0.35 = 0.85$

(c) $P(A/B') = \dfrac{P(A \cap B')}{P(B')} = \dfrac{P(A) - P(A \cap B)}{1 - P(B)} = \dfrac{0.7 - 0.35}{1 - 0.5} = \dfrac{0.35}{0.5} = 0.7$

alternatively, we know that "If A and B are independent then A and B' are also independent",

therefore $P(A/B') = P(A) = 0.7$

(d) $P(A' \cap B) = P(A') \times P(B) = 0.3 \times 0.5 = 0.15$

> ## The Multiplication Principle of Counting
>
> If there are n_1 ways of doing one operation, n_2 ways of doing a second operation, n_3 ways of doing a third operation, and so on, then the sequence of k operations can be performed in N ways, where $N = n_1 \cdot n_2 \cdot n_3 \cdot .... \cdot n_k$

Example

Stelios has 2 pairs of trousers, 2 shirts, and 3 ties. He chooses a pair of trousers, a shirt, and a tie to wear every day. Find the maximum number of days he does not need to repeat his clothing.

Solution

A tree diagram for the above problem is

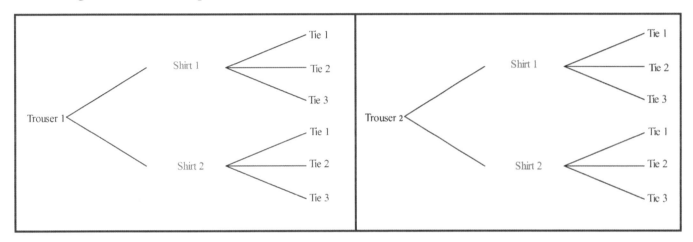

The maximum number of days he does not need to repeat his clothing is:

$$2 \cdot 2 \cdot 3 = 12$$

> ## The Addition Principle of Counting
>
> If there are n_1 ways of doing one operation n_2 ways of doing a second operation, n_3 ways of doing a third operation, and so on, then the first operation or the second operation or the third operation, and so forth, can be performed in N ways where $N = n_1 + n_2 + n_3 + \cdots + n_k$.

Example

Marina can leave an island either by boat **or** by plane. If there are 4 flights and 2 boats leaving the island every day, in how many ways can she leave the island?

Solution

Since Marina can either leave the island by boat **or** by plane (but not both) then by using the addition principle, there are 4+2=6 ways with which she can leave the island.

▪ The product of the first n consecutive integers is denoted by $n!$ and is read as "n factorial"

$$n! = 1 \times 2 \times 3 \times \cdots \times n \ \text{ and } 0! = 1$$

Arrangements

The number of ways of arranging n unlike objects in a line is $n!$.

The number of ways of arranging in a line n objects of which n_1 of one type are alike, n_2 of a second type are alike, n_3 of a third type are alike, and so on, is $\dfrac{n!}{n_1! \times n_2! \times n_3! \times ..}$

Examples

1. In how many ways can the letters of the word JOHN be arranged?

Answer: We have 4 unlike letters, therefore, the answer is 4!=24 ways

2. In how many ways can the letters of the word INVESTMENT be arranged?

Answer: We have 2 E's 2 T's and 2 N's , therefore, the answer is $\dfrac{10!}{2! \times 2! \times 2!} = 453600$ ways

---

Circular Arrangements (Optional)

The total number of arrangements of n unlike objects in a circle is $(n-1)!$

If each object rotates one position either clockwise or counterclockwise, the relative positions remain the same. It still has the same object on its right and the same object on its left.

Example

How many different ways can a family of 6 be seated around a table?

Answer

The total number of arrangements is $(6-1)! = 5! = 120$ ways

Note: Sometimes, the objects on a circular arrangement can be flipped over without creating a different arrangement. Some examples are key rings and beads. This means that there are now half as many arrangements because, for example, flipping a key ring to the opposite side shows a different permutation but does not create a different arrangement of the keys on the ring. The objects can be flipped over without reorganizing them. In this case, the formula would be $\frac{(n-1)!}{2}$.

Examples

1. Four beads, one red, one blue, one black and one white, are threaded on a ring. How many different ways are there to arrange these beads?

Answer

The total number of arrangements is $\frac{(4-1)!}{2} = \frac{3!}{2} = \frac{6}{2} = 3$ ways.

2. Two red, three blue, one black and four white beads are threaded on a ring. How many different ways are there to arrange these beads?

Answer

The total number of arrangements is $\frac{(10-1)!}{2\times2!\times3!\times4!} = \frac{9!}{2\times2\times6\times24} = \frac{362880}{576} = 630$ ways.

Permutations

The total number of ways of arranging n objects, taking r at a time is given by the formula

$$^nP_r = \frac{n!}{(n-r)!}$$

A **permutation** is a selection of a group of objects in which **order is important**.

Example

In how many ways can we select a chairman, vice-chairman, a secretary, and a treasurer from a group of 10 persons?

Answer

The total number of permutations is $^{10}P_4 = \frac{10!}{(10-4)!} = \frac{10!}{6!} = \frac{\cancel{6!} \times 7 \times 8 \times 9 \times 10}{\cancel{6!}} = 5040$ ways.

> ## Combinations
>
> The total number of ways of selecting n objects, taking r at a time is given by the formula
>
> $$\binom{n}{r} = {}^nC_r = \frac{n!}{r! \cdot (n-r)!}$$
>
> Combination is a selection from a group of objects **without regard to order.**

The following example shows the difference between permutations and combinations.

Example

List the different arrangements of three letters that can be chosen from the word CASH. In this case, the order is important.

Answer

Combinations (4)	C,A,S	A,S,H	C,S,H	C,A,H
Permutations (24)	CAS	ASH	CSH	CAH
	CSA	AHS	CHS	CHA
	ASC	SAH	SCH	ACH
	ACS	SHA	SHC	AHC
	SAC	HAS	HCS	HAC
	SCA	HSA	HSC	HCA

There are $^4P_3 = \frac{4!}{(4-3)!} = 4! = 24$ different arrangements.

To find the number of combinations of a three-letter word, where the order is unimportant, divide the total number of permutations by the number of ways, each of three-letter selection can be arranged, i.e.

$$\binom{4}{3} = {}^4C_3 = \frac{4!}{3! \cdot (4-3)!} = 4$$

Discrete Probability Distributions

A **random variable** is called **discrete** if it has either a finite or a countable number of possible values.

A **discrete probability distribution** describes the probability of occurrence of each value of a discrete random variable. The related function that outputs the probabilities of the respective values of the discrete random variable is called a **probability density function (pdf)**.

If X is a **discrete random variable** with $P(X = x_i)$, $i = 1, 2, \ldots n$ then

1. $0 \leq P(X = x_i) \leq 1$ for all values of x_i

2. $\sum_{i=1}^{n} P(X = x_i) = P(X = x_1) + \ldots + P(X = x_n) = 1$

3. The **expectation** of the random variable X is

$$E(X) = \mu = \sum_{i=1}^{n} x_i P(X = x_i)$$

4. The **variance** is defined by the following formula

$$Var(X) = E(X^2) - [E(X)]^2$$

Note: If we have a **fair game** then $E(X) = 0$ where X represents the gain of one of the players.

- For a discrete random variable X, the **mode** is any value of x with the highest probability and it may not be unique.

Example

The following table shows the probability distribution of a discrete random variable X.

x	0	2	4
$P(X = x)$	0.2	$3m$	m

a) Find the value of m
b) Find the expected value of X.

Solution

a) $\sum_{i=1}^{3} P(X = x_i) = 0.2 + 3m + m = 4m + 0.2 \xrightarrow{\text{the sum of probabilities equals 1}} 4m + 0.2 = 1$

$\Rightarrow 4m = 0.8 \Rightarrow m = 0.2$

b) $E(X) = \sum_{i=1}^{3} x_i P(X = x_i) = 0 \times 0.2 + 2 \times (3 \times 0.2) + 4 \times (0.2) = 2$

Binomial Distribution

The **binomial distribution** is a discrete probability distribution. It describes the outcome of n **independent** trials. Each trial is assumed to have only two outcomes, either **success** or **failure**. The probability of a success, denoted by p, remains **constant** from trial to trial. The probability of having exactly r **successes** in n independent trials is given by the following formula:

If a discrete random variable X follows a **Binomial distribution** with parameters $\boldsymbol{n}$ and $\boldsymbol{p}$, $X \sim B(n, p)$, then it has

Expected value (mean)	Variance
$E(X) = np$	$Var(X) = np(1 - p)$

Example

Harry tosses a **fair** coin **seven** times. Calculate the probability of obtaining:

   (i)   Exactly four heads.

   (ii) At least two heads.

Solution

   (i)   Let X denote the number of heads, $X \sim B(7, 0.5)$

$$P(X = 4) = \binom{7}{4}(0.5)^4(0.5)^{7-4} = 0.273 \ (3 \text{ s.f.})$$

   (ii) Let X denote the number of heads, $X \sim B(7, 0.5)$

$$P(X \geq 2) = 1 - P(X \leq 1) = 1 - \big(P(X = 0) + P(X = 1)\big) = 0.938 (3 \text{ s.f.})$$

where $P(X = 0) = \binom{7}{0}(0.5)^0(0.5)^{7-0} = 0.00781 (3 \text{ s.f.})$

$$P(X = 1) = \binom{7}{1}(0.5)^1(0.5)^{7-1} = 0.0546875$$

TI 84 + (Example)		CASIO fx9860 series, fx-CG20, fx-CG50 (Example)	
$X{\sim}B(7,0.5)$ $P(X=4)$	**binompdf**$(numtrials, p, x)$ Computes a probability at x for the discrete binomial distribution with the specified *numtrials* and probability p of success on each trial. 2nd [DISTR] **DISTR** **A:binompdf(7,0.5,4)**	$X{\sim}B(7,0.5)$ $P(X=4)$	On the initial STAT mode screen$\rightarrow$F5(DIST)$\rightarrow$F5(BINM)$\rightarrow$F1(Bpd) we set Data: **Variable**, x: **4**, Numtrial: **7**, p: **0.5**$\rightarrow$Execute $P(X=4)=0.273\ (3\,\mathrm{s.f.})$
$X{\sim}B(7,0.5)$ $P(X\le 1)$	**binomcdf**$(numtrials, p, x)$ Computes a cumulative probability at x for the discrete binomial distribution with the specified *numtrials* and probability p of success on each trial. 2nd [DISTR] **DISTR** **B:binomcdf(7,0.5,1)**	$X{\sim}B(7,0.5)$ $P(X\le 1)$	On the initial STAT mode screen$\rightarrow$F5(DIST)$\rightarrow$F5(BINM)$\rightarrow$F2(Bcd) we set Data: **Variable**, x: **1**, Numtrial: **7**, p: **0.5**$\rightarrow$Execute $P(X\le 1)=0.063$ and then $P(X\ge 2)=1-P(X\le 1)=0.938(3\,\mathrm{s.f.})$

Note: CASIO models **fx-CG20**, **fx-CG50** calculate directly the probability $P(X\ge 2)$.

Poisson Distribution

The **Poisson distribution** is a discrete probability distribution. The Poisson distribution is used to model the number of events occurring within a given time interval. The probability of success during a small time interval is proportional to the entire length of the time interval. The number of successes in two disjoint time intervals is independent. The probability distribution of a Poisson random variable X representing the number of events occurring in a fixed interval of time and/or space is given by the following formula:

$$P(X = x) = \frac{m^x e^{-m}}{x!}$$

Where m is a parameter which indicates the average number of events in the given time interval and $x = 0, 1, ...$

If a discrete random variable X follows a Poisson distribution with parameter m, written $X \sim Po(m)$, then it has

Expected value (mean)	Variance
$E(X) = m$	$Var(X) = m$

Example

Cars pass through a road junction according to a Poisson distribution. The probability of one or more cars passing through the road junction during one hour is 0.36. What is the probability of a car passing through the road junction during the next half hour?

Solution

1st method

Let the random variable C denote the number of cars passing through the road junction **during one hour.** Then, we have that $C \sim Po(m)$ where m is unknown.

We know that $P(C \geq 1) = 0.36$

So, $1 - P(C = 0) = 0.36 \Rightarrow P(C = 0) = 1 - 0.36 \Rightarrow P(C = 0) = 0.64 \Rightarrow \frac{m^0 e^{-m}}{0!} = 0.64 \Rightarrow$

$$e^{-m} = 0.64$$

Let the random variable Y denote the number of cars passing through the road junction **during a half-hour period.** Then, we have that $Y \sim Po\left(\frac{m}{2}\right)$. We want to find the probability $P(Y \geq 1)$.

$$P(Y \geq 1) = 1 - P(Y = 0) = 1 - \frac{\left(\frac{m}{2}\right)^0 e^{-\frac{m}{2}}}{0!} = 1 - e^{-\frac{m}{2}} = 1 - (e^{-m})^{\frac{1}{2}} = 1 - \sqrt{0.64} = 0.2$$

2nd method

Let q be the probability of no car passing through the road junction during the next half hour. Due to the property of the Poisson distribution that says «the number of successes in two disjoint time intervals is independent», the probability of no car passing through the road junction during one hour is q^2.

We know that $q^2 = 1 - 0.36 = 0.64$, therefore $q = 0.8$.

So, the probability of a car passing through the road junction during the next half hour is:

$$1 - q = 1 - 0.8 = 0.2$$

TI 84 + (Example)		CASIO fx9860 series, fx-CG20, fx-CG50 (Example)	
$X \sim Po(5)$ $P(X = 1)$	**poissoncdf**(m, x) Computes a probability at x for the discrete Poisson distribution with mean m. 2nd [DISTR] **DISTR** **C:poissonpdf(5,1)**	$X \sim Po(5)$ $P(X = 1)$	On the initial STAT mode screen→F5(DIST)→F6(▶)→F1(POISN) →F1(Ppd) we set Data: **Variable, x: 1, μ: 5**→Execute
$X \sim Po(5)$ $P(X \leq 1)$	**poissoncdf**(m, x) Computes a cumulative probability at x for the discrete Poisson distribution with mean m. 2nd [DISTR] **DISTR** **D:poissoncdf(5,1)**	$X \sim Po(5)$ $P(X \leq 1)$	On the initial STAT mode screen→F5(DIST)→F6(▶)→F1(POISN) →F2(Pcd) we set Data: **Variable, x: 1, μ: 5**→Execute

Note: Casio models **fx-CG20, fx-CG50 calculate directly the probability** $P(X \geq 2)$ without the need to calculate first $P(X \leq 1)$ and then find $P(X \geq 2)$ by the following formula $P(X \geq 2) = 1 - P(X \leq 1)$.

Probability density functions

A **continuous random variable** is a random variable which can take values measured on a continuous scale e.g. heights, weights, lengths or times. For every value x, $P(X = x) = 0$, no matter how accurately we measure X, we are never going to hit the value x exactly.

> Any real-valued function $f(x)$ that satisfies:
> $$f(x) \geq 0 \text{ for every } x \in \mathbb{R}$$
> $$\text{and } \int_{-\infty}^{+\infty} f(x)dx = 1$$
> is a valid Probability Density Function (PDF)

$$P(a \leq X \leq b) = P(a < X < b) = P(a \leq X < b) = P(a < X \leq b) = \int_a^b f(x)\, dx$$

If X is a **continuous random variable** with probability density function $f(x)$ then the **expected value (mean) of** X is defined as follows:

$$E(X) = \mu = \int_{-\infty}^{+\infty} xf(x)dx$$

the **variance** is defined by the following formula

$$Var(X) = E(X^2) - [E(X)]^2 = \int_{-\infty}^{+\infty} (x-\mu)^2 f(x)dx = \int_{-\infty}^{+\infty} x^2 f(x)dx - \mu^2$$

the **standard deviation** σ is defined as follows:

$$\sigma = \sqrt{Var(X)}$$

The **median** m of a random variable X, that has a probability density function $f(x)$, is a value of x such that

$$\int_{-\infty}^{m} f(x)dx = \frac{1}{2}$$

▨ The **percentiles** can be found in a similar way.

Let p be a number between 0 and 1. The $(100p)th$ percentile of the distribution of a continuous random variable X, denoted by P_i, is defined as follows:

$$p = \int_{-\infty}^{P_i} f(x)dx$$

where P_i is the specific value such that the $100p\%$ of the area under the area of $f(x)$ lies to the left of P_i and the $100(1-p)\%$ lies to the right.

▨ The **mode** is a measure of the most likely value occurring of the random variable X.

Thus, we require a value of x for which the probability density function $f(x)$ has a maximum.

To determine the mode, you may use calculus to find the maximum.

▨ The **Cumulative Distribution Function (CDF)** of a random variable X is defined by

$$F(x) = P(X \le x) = \int_{-\infty}^{x} f(t)dt$$

where the function $f(x)$ is the probability density function of the random variable X.

Example

Let $f(x) = \begin{cases} ke^{-4x} & \text{for } 1 \le x \le 3 \\ 0 & \text{otherwise} \end{cases}$

(i)   Find the constant k.

(ii)   Find $P(2 \le X < 3)$.

(iii)   Find the mean, mode, median, and interquartile range of the random variable X.

Solution

(i)   We need $\int_{-\infty}^{+\infty} f(x)dx = 1 \Rightarrow \int_{-\infty}^{1} f(x)dx + \int_{1}^{3} f(x)dx + \int_{3}^{+\infty} f(x)dx = 1$

$$\Rightarrow 0 + \int_{1}^{3} ke^{-4x}dx + 0 = 1 \Rightarrow k\int_{1}^{3} e^{-4x}dx = 1 \Rightarrow k\left[\frac{e^{-4x}}{-4}\right]_{1}^{3} = 1$$

$$\Rightarrow k\left[\frac{e^{-4x}}{-4}\right]_{1}^{3} = 1 \Rightarrow \frac{k}{-4}\left(e^{-4(3)} - e^{-4(1)}\right) = 1 \Rightarrow k(e^{-12} - e^{-4}) = -4$$

$$\Rightarrow k = \frac{-4}{(e^{-12} - e^{-4})}$$

(ii) $P(2 \le X < 3) = \int_{2}^{3} ke^{-4x}dx = \int_{2}^{3} \frac{-4}{(e^{-12}-e^{-4})}e^{-4x}dx = \frac{-4}{(e^{-12}-e^{-4})}\left[\frac{e^{-4x}}{-4}\right]_{2}^{3} =$

$$= \frac{1}{(e^{-12} - e^{-4})}(e^{-12} - e^{-8}) = 0.01798 = 0.0180 \ (3 \ s.f.)$$

(iii) Mean: $E(X) = \int_{-\infty}^{+\infty} xf(x)dx = \int_1^3 \frac{-4x}{(e^{-12}-e^{-4})}e^{-4x}dx = 1.24932 = 1.25 \ (3 \ s.f.)$

Mode: $f(x) = \begin{cases} \frac{-4e^{-4x}}{(e^{-12}-e^{-4})} & for \ 1 \le x \le 3 \\ 0 & otherwise \end{cases}$

$f_{max}(x) = f(1)$ since $f(x)$ is a strictly decreasing function, so the **mode** is at $x = 1$

Median **(m)**: $\int_{-\infty}^{m} f(x)dx = \frac{1}{2} \Rightarrow \int_1^m \frac{-4e^{-4x}}{(e^{-12}-e^{-4})}dx = \frac{1}{2} \xrightarrow{by \ using \ GDC} m = 1.17 \ (3 \ s.f.)$

Lower Quartile **(Q_1)**: $\int_{-\infty}^{Q_1} f(x)dx = \frac{1}{4} \Rightarrow \int_1^{Q_1} \frac{-4e^{-4x}}{(e^{-12}-e^{-4})}dx = \frac{1}{4} \xrightarrow{by \ using \ GDC} Q_1 = 1.07 \ (3 \ s.f.)$

Upper Quartile **(Q_3)**: $\int_{-\infty}^{Q_3} f(x)dx = \frac{3}{4} \Rightarrow \int_1^{Q_3} \frac{-4e^{-4x}}{(e^{-12}-e^{-4})}dx = \frac{3}{4} \xrightarrow{by \ using \ GDC} Q_3 = 1.35 \ (3 \ s.f.)$

Interquartile range: $IQR = Q_3 - Q_1 = 1.34632 - 1.07189 = 0.27443 = 0.274 \ (3 \ s.f.)$

Normal Distribution

The **normal distribution** is a theoretical ideal distribution. Real-life empirical distributions never match this model perfectly. However, many things in life do approximate the normal distribution, and are said to be "normally distributed".

The normal distribution has the following properties:

▨   Its shape is symmetric about the **mean** (μ), which is also the **median** and the **mode** of the distribution.

▨   It is a bell-shaped curve, with tails going down and out to the left and right and the x-axis is a horizontal asymptote.

▨   Its standard deviation (σ), measures the distance on the distribution from the mean to the inflection point.

▨   The total area under the curve is equal to 1.

▨   Approximately 68 percent of its values lie within one standard deviation of the mean.

▨   Approximately 95 percent of its values lie within two standard deviations of the mean.

▨   Approximately 99.7 percent of them lie within three standard deviations of the mean.

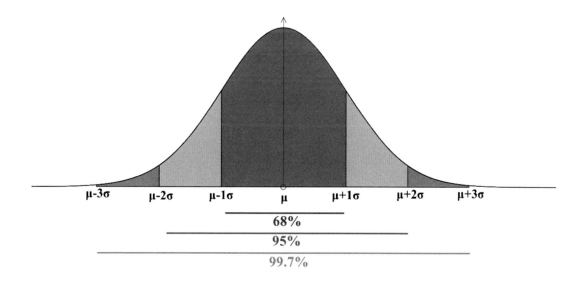

Example

The weights of a group of men are normally distributed with a mean of 80 kg and a standard deviation of 15 kg.

(i)   A man is chosen at random. Find the probability that the man's weight is greater than 90 kg.

(ii)   In this group, 20% of men weigh less than w kg. Find the value of w.

Solution

The required probability for **(i)** is represented in the following diagram.

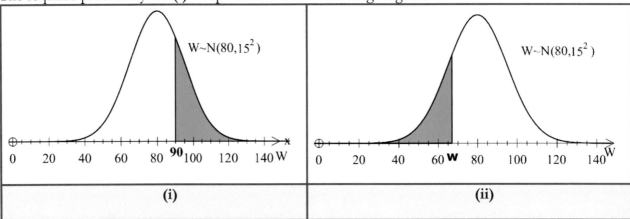

| (i) | (ii) |

In order to find this probability, we can use GDC.

▨ For **Casio fx9860 series, fx-CG20, fx-CG50**, we perform the following commands:

On the initial STAT mode screen→F5(DIST)→F1(NORM)→F2(Ncd)

we set Lower: **90**, Upper: **10^99**, σ: **15**, μ: **80**→ Execute

$$P(W > 90) = 0.252 \text{ (3 s. f.)}$$

▨ For **TI 84 +**

2nd→VARS→2→Enter four parameters (lower limit: **90**, upper limit: **10^99**, mean: **80**, standard deviation: **15**)

(ii) In order to find the value of w, we have to use the inverse normal, which gives us an x-value if we input the area (probability region) to the left of the x-value.

In order to find this probability, we can use GDC.

▨ For **Casio fx9860 series, fx-CG20, fx-CG50**

On the initial STAT mode screen→F5(DIST)→F1(NORM)→F3(InvN)

we set Tail: Left, Area(probability less than): **0.20**, σ: **15**, μ: **80**→Execute

▨ For **TI 84 +**

2nd→VARS→3→Enter three parameters (probability less than - area: **90**, mean: **80**, standard deviation: **15**)

$$P(W < w) = 0.20 \Rightarrow w = 67.4$$

Important: There are many normal distribution exercises where we have to find the **mean(μ)** and/or the **standard deviation (σ)**. In this case, we have to convert this normal distribution $X \sim N(\mu, \sigma^2)$ to a standard normal distribution $Z \sim N(0, 1^2)$ by using the formula $Z = \dfrac{x - \mu}{\sigma}$.

Vectors

A **vector** is an object that has both a **magnitude** and a **direction**.

Magnitude is defined as the length of a vector

$$|a| = \left|\binom{a_1}{a_2}\right| = \sqrt{a_1{}^2 + a_2{}^2} \quad \textbf{(2D)}$$

$$|a| = \left|\begin{pmatrix} a_1 \\ a_2 \\ a_3 \end{pmatrix}\right| = \sqrt{a_1{}^2 + a_2{}^2 + a_3{}^2} \quad \textbf{(3D)}$$

The zero vector **0** has zero magnitude, $|\mathbf{0}| = 0$ and has no definite direction.

Two vectors are **equal** if they have the same magnitude and direction.

Two vectors are **parallel** if they have the same direction or are in exactly opposite directions.

Two vectors are **parallel** if one is a scalar multiple of the other $(k\epsilon\mathbb{R})$.

$$a \parallel b \Leftrightarrow a = kb$$

A **unit vector** is a vector that has a magnitude of 1.

Any vector a can become a **unit vector** $\hat{a}$ by dividing it by its magnitude, i.e. $\hat{a} = \frac{a}{|a|}$.

The unit vectors i, j and k are also known as the **base unit vectors** of x, y and z-axis respectively.

$$i = \begin{pmatrix} 1 \\ 0 \\ 0 \end{pmatrix}, j = \begin{pmatrix} 0 \\ 1 \\ 0 \end{pmatrix}, k = \begin{pmatrix} 0 \\ 0 \\ 1 \end{pmatrix}$$

For example, the vector $a = \begin{pmatrix} -2 \\ 5 \\ 4 \end{pmatrix}$ can also be written as $a = -2i + 5j + 4k$

Operations on Vectors

Vector Addition

The sum of two vectors a and b is defined as the diagonal of the parallelogram formed when the two vectors a and b are placed at the same point, as is described in the following diagram.

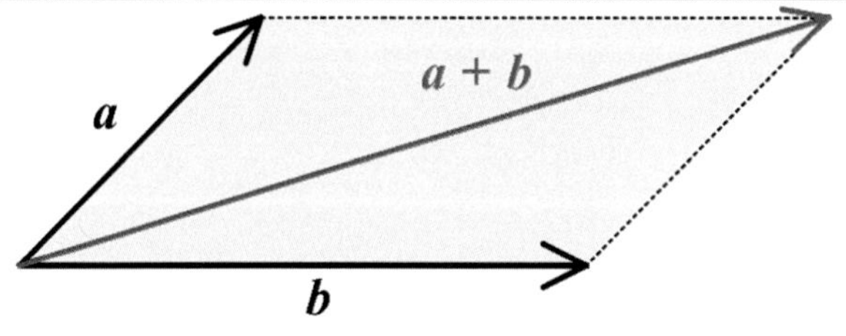

$$a + b = \binom{a_1}{a_2} + \binom{b_1}{b_2} = \binom{a_1 + b_1}{a_2 + b_2} \textbf{(2D)}$$

$$a + b = \begin{pmatrix} a_1 \\ a_2 \\ a_3 \end{pmatrix} + \begin{pmatrix} b_1 \\ b_2 \\ b_3 \end{pmatrix} = \begin{pmatrix} a_1 + b_1 \\ a_2 + b_2 \\ a_3 + b_3 \end{pmatrix} \textbf{(3D)}$$

The negative of a vector

The vector $-a$ is defined to be the same as vector a, but with the opposite direction and $a + (-a) = 0$

The negative of $\overrightarrow{AB}$ is $-\overrightarrow{AB}$ or $\overrightarrow{BA}$.

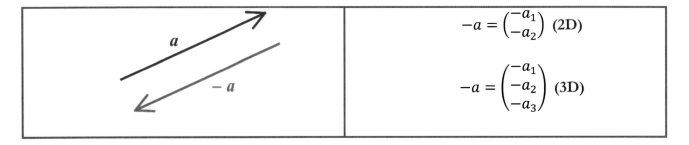

$$-a = \begin{pmatrix} -a_1 \\ -a_2 \end{pmatrix} \text{ (2D)}$$

$$-a = \begin{pmatrix} -a_1 \\ -a_2 \\ -a_3 \end{pmatrix} \text{ (3D)}$$

Vector subtraction

Vector subtraction $a - b$ is defined as:

$a + (-b)$, that is, adding the negative of the subtracted vector b.

$$a - b = \begin{pmatrix} a_1 \\ a_2 \end{pmatrix} - \begin{pmatrix} b_1 \\ b_2 \end{pmatrix} = \begin{pmatrix} a_1 - b_1 \\ a_2 - b_2 \end{pmatrix} \text{ (2D)}$$

$$a - b = \begin{pmatrix} a_1 \\ a_2 \\ a_3 \end{pmatrix} - \begin{pmatrix} b_1 \\ b_2 \\ b_3 \end{pmatrix} = \begin{pmatrix} a_1 - b_1 \\ a_2 - b_2 \\ a_3 - b_3 \end{pmatrix} \text{ (3D)}$$

The vector between two points

If A, B are two points with position vectors $\overrightarrow{OA} = \begin{pmatrix} a_1 \\ a_2 \\ a_3 \end{pmatrix}, \overrightarrow{OB} = \begin{pmatrix} b_1 \\ b_2 \\ b_3 \end{pmatrix}$ respectively, then the position

vector of B relative to A is $\overrightarrow{AB} = \overrightarrow{OB} - \overrightarrow{OA} = \begin{pmatrix} b_1 \\ b_2 \\ b_3 \end{pmatrix} - \begin{pmatrix} a_1 \\ a_2 \\ a_3 \end{pmatrix} = \begin{pmatrix} b_1 - a_1 \\ b_2 - a_2 \\ b_3 - a_3 \end{pmatrix}$

Multiplication by a scalar

Multiplying a vector a by a scalar k gives a new vector with the same direction but with a magnitude which is multiplied by this scalar.

$$ka = k \begin{pmatrix} a_1 \\ a_2 \\ a_3 \end{pmatrix} = \begin{pmatrix} ka_1 \\ ka_2 \\ ka_3 \end{pmatrix}$$

Scalar Product

The **scalar product** or **dot product** can be defined for two vectors $\boldsymbol{a}$ and $\boldsymbol{b}$ by

$$a \cdot b = |a||b|cos\theta$$

$$cos\theta = \frac{a \cdot b}{|a||b|}$$

where θ is the **angle** between the vectors and $|a|, |b|$ are the **magnitudes** (lengths) of each vector.

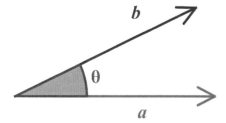

If the vectors are expressed in component form, the **dot product** can also be expressed in the following forms:

$\begin{pmatrix} a_1 \\ a_2 \end{pmatrix} \cdot \begin{pmatrix} b_1 \\ b_2 \end{pmatrix} = a_1b_1 + a_2b_2$ **(2D)**	$\begin{pmatrix} a_1 \\ a_2 \\ a_3 \end{pmatrix} \cdot \begin{pmatrix} b_1 \\ b_2 \\ b_3 \end{pmatrix} = a_1b_1 + a_2b_2 + a_3b_3$ **(3D)**

Properties of Scalar Product

If a, b, c are vectors and k is a scalar then

1. $a \cdot b = b \cdot a$

2. $a \cdot a = |a|^2$

3. $a \cdot (b + c) = a \cdot b + a \cdot c$

4. $(ka) \cdot b = k(a \cdot b) = a \cdot (kb)$

5. $\mathbf{0} \cdot a = 0$

▦ If two vectors are **perpendicular** then,

$$a \cdot b = 0$$

▦ If two vectors are **parallel** then,

$$a \cdot b = |a||b|cos0^o = |a||b|$$

or

$$a \cdot b = |a||b|cos180^o = -|a||b|$$

Vector Projection

The **scalar projection** of b onto a is the magnitude of the vector $proj_a b$ shown in the figure below. The **vector projection** of b onto a is the vector $proj_a b$.

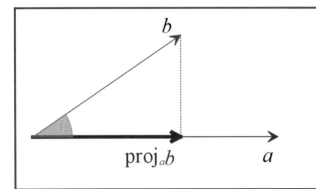

$$|proj_a b| = b \cdot \hat{a} = \frac{a \cdot b}{|a|}$$

$$proj_a b = (b \cdot \hat{a})\hat{a} = \frac{a \cdot b}{|a|}\frac{a}{|a|} = \frac{a \cdot b}{|a|^2}a$$

Cross Product

The **cross product** or **vector product** can be defined for two vectors a and b by

$$a \times b = |a||b|sin\theta\hat{n}$$

where θ is the **angle** between the vectors, $|a|, |b|$ are the **magnitudes** (lengths) of each vector and $\hat{n}$ is the unit normal vector (at right angles to both a and b).

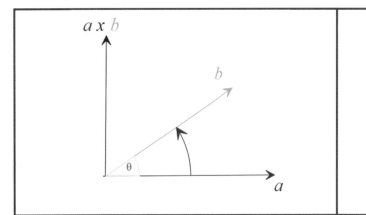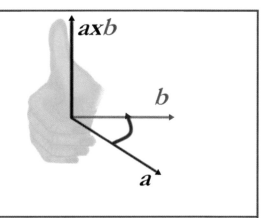

The direction of the cross product vector $a \times b$, is what your thumb points as the fingers on your right hand curl from a to b.

| $i \times j = k$ | $j \times i = -k$ | $k \times j = -i$ | $i \times k = -j$ | $j \times k = i$ | $k \times i = j$ |

■   If the vectors are expressed in component form, the **cross product** can also be expressed in the following form:

$$\begin{pmatrix} a_1 \\ a_2 \\ a_3 \end{pmatrix} \times \begin{pmatrix} b_1 \\ b_2 \\ b_3 \end{pmatrix} = \begin{pmatrix} a_2 b_3 - a_3 b_2 \\ a_3 b_1 - a_1 b_3 \\ a_1 b_2 - a_2 b_1 \end{pmatrix}$$

Properties of Cross Product

If a, b, c are vectors and k is a scalar then

1. $a \times b = -b \times a$

2. $(ka) \times b = k(a \times b) = a \times (kb)$

3. $a \times (b + c) = a \times b + a \times c$

4. $(a + b) \times c = a \times c + b \times c$

5. $a \cdot (b \times c) = (a \times b) \cdot c$

6. $a \times (b \times c) = (a \cdot c)b - (a \cdot b)c$

7. $|a \times b| = |a||b|sin\theta$

8. $a \times a = \mathbf{0}$

■   Two non-zero vectors a and b are parallel if and only if $a \times b = \mathbf{0}$

Applications of the Cross Product

■   The **area of a triangle** defined by the vectors a and b, is determined by the following formula:

$$A = \frac{1}{2}|a \times b|$$

■   The **area of a parallelogram** defined by the vectors a and b, is determined by the following formula:

$$A = |a \times b|$$

■   The **volume of a parallelepiped** defined by the vectors a, b and c, is determined by the following formula:

$$V = |a \cdot (b \times c)|$$

▦ The **volume of a tetrahedron** (pyramid) defined by the vectors a, b and c, is determined by the following formula:

$$V = \frac{|a \cdot (b \times c)|}{6}$$

Lines

Vector equation of a line

$$r = a + \lambda b$$

where a is a **position vector** (a point which lies on the line), b the **direction vector** (a vector parallel to the line) and $\lambda \in \mathbb{R}$ is called the **parameter**.

The parametric form of the equation of a line

$$x = a_1 + \lambda b_1$$
$$y = a_2 + \lambda b_2$$
$$z = a_3 + \lambda b_3$$

where $a = \begin{pmatrix} a_1 \\ a_2 \\ a_3 \end{pmatrix}$ is a **position vector**, $b = \begin{pmatrix} b_1 \\ b_2 \\ b_3 \end{pmatrix}$ the **direction vector** of the line and $\lambda \in \mathbb{R}$ is called the **parameter**.

Cartesian equations of a line

$$\frac{x - a_1}{b_1} = \frac{y - a_2}{b_2} = \frac{z - a_3}{b_3}$$

where $a = \begin{pmatrix} a_1 \\ a_2 \\ a_3 \end{pmatrix}$ is a position vector and $b = \begin{pmatrix} b_1 \\ b_2 \\ b_3 \end{pmatrix}$ the direction vector of the line.

Note: The acute angle θ between two lines l_1, l_2 can be found by using the following formula

$$\cos\theta = \frac{|b \cdot c|}{|b||c|}$$

where b, c are the direction vectors of the lines l_1 and l_2 respectively.

Relative Positions of two Lines

In 2-D or 3-D

▦ **Intersecting lines** meet at a unique point.

▦ **Perpendicular lines** have their direction vectors perpendicular, i.e. their dot product equals zero.

▦ **Parallel lines** are lines that never touch. Their direction vectors are parallel (scalar multiples of one another).

▦ **Skew lines** (only in 3D) are lines that do not intersect and are not parallel.

▦ **Coincident (identical) lines** are lines that lie exactly on top of each other. These lines are parallel and meet at a point. So, they are the same line.

Example

Find the point of intersection between the lines defined by the following two equations:

$$L_1: r = \begin{pmatrix} 1 \\ 0 \\ 3 \end{pmatrix} + \lambda \begin{pmatrix} -1 \\ 1 \\ -2 \end{pmatrix} \qquad\qquad L_2: r = \begin{pmatrix} 1 \\ -1 \\ 4 \end{pmatrix} + \mu \begin{pmatrix} 2 \\ -1 \\ 3 \end{pmatrix}$$

The parametric form of these lines is:

$$L_1: x = 1 - \lambda, \qquad y = \lambda, \qquad z = 3 - 2\lambda$$

$$L_2: x = 1 + 2\mu, \qquad y = -1 - \mu, \qquad z = 4 + 3\mu$$

For the lines to intersect, there must be a value of λ and μ that will provide the same point lying on both L_1 and L_2. Using the parametric equations, we equate the coordinates and try to determine the common point.

$$1 - \lambda = 1 + 2\mu \quad (1)$$
$$\lambda = -1 - \mu \quad (2)$$
$$3 - 2\lambda = 4 + 3\mu \quad (3)$$

Solving for λ and μ using (1) and (2) we obtain: $\lambda = -2$ and $\mu = 1$.

Checking these values in (3), we have $3 - 2(-2) = 7 = 4 + 3(1)$

Using $\lambda = -2$ or $\mu = 1$,

$$x = 1 - (-2) = 3, \qquad y = -2, \qquad z = 3 - 2(-2) = 7$$

we can determine the point of intersection $(3, -2, 7)$.

Planes

▣ Vector equation of a plane

$$r = a + \lambda b + \mu c$$

where a is a position vector (a point which lies on the plane), b, c are two non-parallel vectors in the plane and λ, μ are scalar parameters $(\lambda, \mu \in \mathbb{R})$.

▣ Equation of a plane using the normal vector

$$r \cdot n = a \cdot n$$

where $a = \begin{pmatrix} a_1 \\ a_2 \\ a_3 \end{pmatrix}$ is a position vector of the plane and $n = \begin{pmatrix} n_1 \\ n_2 \\ n_3 \end{pmatrix}$ a normal vector of the line.

Another expression of the previous equation is

$$r \cdot \hat{n} = D$$

where $\hat{n}$ is the unit normal and D is the distance of the plane from the origin.

▣ Cartesian equation of a plane

$$ax + by + cz = d$$

where the vector $n = \begin{pmatrix} a \\ b \\ c \end{pmatrix}$ is a normal to this plane.

Example

Find the point of intersection of the line $L: r = \begin{pmatrix} 1 \\ -2 \\ 4 \end{pmatrix} + \lambda \begin{pmatrix} 1 \\ 3 \\ -5 \end{pmatrix}$ and the plane $\Pi: 2x + y + 3z = 2$.

Solution

The parametric equations of the line L are given below

$$L_1: x = 1 + \lambda, \qquad y = -2 + 3\lambda, \qquad z = 4 - 5\lambda$$

Substituting each of these expressions into the equation of the plane Π we obtain

$$2(1 + \lambda) + (-2 + 3\lambda) + 3(4 - 5\lambda) = 2$$

Then we expand and solve for the parameter λ

$$2 + 2\lambda - 2 + 3\lambda + 12 - 15\lambda = 2 \Rightarrow -10\lambda = -10 \Rightarrow \lambda = 1$$

Since a single value of λ was found, the line and the plane intersect at exactly one point. Substitute $\lambda = -1$ in the parametric equations

$$x = 1 + (1) = 2, \qquad y = -2 + 3(1) = 1, \qquad z = 4 - 5(1) = -1$$

The line and the plane intersect at the point $(2, 1, -1)$.

▨   The **angle φ** between a line l with equation $r = u + \lambda v$ and a plane Π with normal n is $90° - \vartheta$, where ϑ is the acute angle between the direction vector v and normal n.

$$\varphi = 90° - \vartheta = 90° - arccos\left(\frac{|v \cdot n|}{|v||n|}\right)$$

▨   The **acute angle φ** between two planes (Π_1, Π_2) is equal to the acute angle between their normals (n_1, n_2).

$$\varphi = arccos\left(\frac{|n_1 \cdot n_2|}{|n_1||n_2|}\right)$$

▨   A **direction vector v** of the line of intersection of two planes (Π_1, Π_2) is given by the cross product of their normals (n_1, n_2).

$$v = n_1 \times n_2$$

■   The **distance from a point** $P(x_0, y_0, z_0)$ to a **plane** $\Pi: ax + by + cz = d$ is given by the scalar projection of the vector $\overrightarrow{AP}$ onto the normal vector $\vec{n}$, where $A(x_A, y_A, z_A)$ a point on this plane.

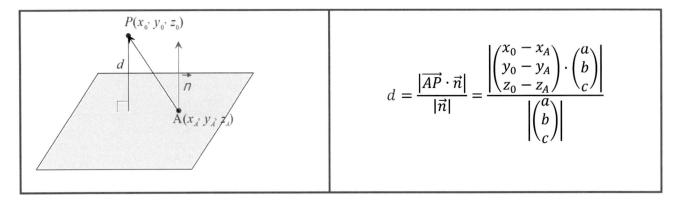

■   To find the distance between two parallel planes:

1)   Choose a certain point into one of these two planes

2)   Then find the distance between that point and the other plane using the formula above.

■   To find the distance between two skew lines l_1, l_2:

1)   Find an equation of the plane containing the line l_1 (with direction vector b_1) and a parallel to the line l_2 (with direction vector b_2). A normal vector n to this plane should be perpendicular to both b_1 and b_2. Thus in order to find the normal vector n, we use the cross product,

$$n = b_1 \times b_2$$

We already have found a normal vector, so we only need a point. We can choose any point from the line l_1 and finally, obtain the equation of the plane.

2)   To find the distance between these two skew lines, all we need to do is find the distance from any point on l_2 to the plane which is found in the previous step.

Two planes	Three planes
Intersect along a line (non-parallel normal vectors)	Intersect along a line
Do not intersect (parallel normal vectors)	Intersect at a unique point
Coincide (parallel normal vectors and one common point)	Intersect in a plane
	Do not intersect

Gauss-Jordan elimination method

The **Gauss-Jordan elimination method** to solve a system of linear equations is described in the following steps:

1. Write the augmented matrix of the system. (To express a system in matrix form, we extract the coefficients of the variables and the constants, and these become the entries of the augmented matrix)

2. Use row operations to transform the augmented matrix in the reduced row echelon form (RREF).

We say that a matrix A is in reduced row-echelon form if the following conditions hold for A:

- Each non-zero row has first non-zero entry equal to 1.

- If a column contains an entry equal to 1, then every other entry in the column is zero.

- The leading 1 in any row is to the left of any leading 1's in the rows below it.

- All zero rows are at the bottom.

The **three types of elementary row operations** are the following:

1. Add a multiple of one row to another row.

2. Multiply a row by a non-zero constant c.

3. Interchange two rows.

Example

Solve the following simultaneous equations by using Gaussian elimination

$$\begin{cases} 2y + z = -8 \\ x - 2y - 3z = 0 \\ -x + y + 2z = 3 \end{cases}$$

$$\begin{pmatrix} 0 & 2 & 1 & -8 \\ 1 & -2 & -3 & 0 \\ -1 & 1 & 2 & 3 \end{pmatrix} \xrightarrow{\text{Swap Row 1 and Row 2}} \begin{pmatrix} 1 & -2 & -3 & 0 \\ 0 & 2 & 1 & -8 \\ -1 & 1 & 2 & 3 \end{pmatrix} \xrightarrow{\text{Add Row 1 to Row 3}}$$

$$\begin{pmatrix} 1 & -2 & -3 & 0 \\ 0 & 2 & 1 & -8 \\ 0 & -1 & -1 & 3 \end{pmatrix} \xrightarrow{\text{Swap Row 2 and Row 3}} \begin{pmatrix} 1 & -2 & -3 & 0 \\ 0 & -1 & -1 & 3 \\ 0 & 2 & 1 & -8 \end{pmatrix} \xrightarrow{\text{Add twice Row 2 to Row 3}}$$

$$\begin{pmatrix} 1 & -2 & -3 & 0 \\ 0 & -1 & -1 & 3 \\ 0 & 0 & -1 & -2 \end{pmatrix} \xrightarrow{\text{Add } -1 \text{ times Row 3 to Row 2}} \begin{pmatrix} 1 & -2 & -3 & 0 \\ 0 & -1 & 0 & 5 \\ 0 & 0 & -1 & -2 \end{pmatrix} \xrightarrow{\text{Add } -3 \text{ times Row 3 to Row 1}}$$

$$\begin{pmatrix} 1 & -2 & 0 & 6 \\ 0 & -1 & 0 & 5 \\ 0 & 0 & -1 & -2 \end{pmatrix} \xrightarrow{\text{Add } -2 \text{ times Row 2 to Row 1}} \begin{pmatrix} 1 & 0 & 0 & -4 \\ 0 & -1 & 0 & 5 \\ 0 & 0 & -1 & -2 \end{pmatrix} \xrightarrow{\text{Multiply Rows 2 and 3 by} -1}$$

$$\begin{pmatrix} 1 & 0 & 0 & -4 \\ 0 & 1 & 0 & -5 \\ 0 & 0 & 1 & 2 \end{pmatrix} \xrightarrow{\text{The last matrix give us the unique solution}} \begin{cases} x = -4 \\ y = -5 \\ z = 2 \end{cases}$$

Determinant method

A **determinant** is a value associated with a square matrix (same number of rows and columns).

The determinant of a 2×2 matrix A is defined as follows:

$$A = \begin{pmatrix} a & b \\ c & d \end{pmatrix} \Rightarrow \det(A) = |A| = ad - bc$$

The determinant of a 3×3 matrix A is defined as follows:

$$A = \begin{pmatrix} a & b & c \\ d & e & f \\ g & h & k \end{pmatrix} \Rightarrow \det(A) = |A| = aek + bfg + cdh - ceg - afh - bdk$$

The determinant of a matrix A is usually denoted $|A|$ or $\det(A)$.

If the determinant of a matrix A, whose entries are the coefficients in a system of linear equations, equals zero $(\det(A) = 0)$, then the system has either no solutions or infinitely many solutions. Otherwise $(\det(A) \neq 0)$ the system has one unique solution.

Note: The expressions of the determinant of a 2×2 and 3×3 matrices are included in the formula booklet on page 14.

Example

Consider the following system of equations:
$$\begin{cases} 2x + 2y + 2z = 2 \\ 4x + 6y + 2z = 6 \\ 2x + 6y - 2z = b \end{cases}$$

where $b \in \mathbb{R}$. Show that the above system does not have a unique solution for any value of b.

Solution

The determinant of the matrix $A = \begin{pmatrix} 2 & 2 & 2 \\ 4 & 6 & 2 \\ 2 & 6 & -2 \end{pmatrix}$ is $|A| = (2)(6)(-2) + (2)(2)(2) + (2)(4)(6) -$

$(2)(6)(2) - (2)(2)(6) - (2)(4)(-2) = -24 + 8 + 48 - 24 - 24 + 16 = 0$

Therefore, **the system does not have a unique solution.**

Kinematics

An important application of vectors is on kinematics.

The vector equation

$$r = a + tb$$

represents the position of a particle at **time** t, where a is its **initial position** and b is its **velocity vector**.

The **speed** of the particle is the magnitude of the **velocity vector** $|b|$.

Example

Let $r = \binom{1}{2} + t\binom{5}{6}$ the vector equation of the motion of a particle, where t represents the time in seconds and distances are measured in meters.

(a)   Find the particle's initial position.

(b)   Find the velocity vector of the particle.

(c)   Find the speed of the particle.

Solution

(a)   The initial position is when $t = 0$, so $r = \binom{1}{2}$.

(b)   The velocity vector is $\binom{5}{6}$.

(c)   Speed (s) is the magnitude of velocity, thus $s = \left|\binom{5}{6}\right| = \sqrt{5^2 + 6^2} = \sqrt{61}\, ms^{-1}$.

Complex Numbers

Any number of the form $a + ib$ where a and b are real and $i = \sqrt{-1}$ is called a **complex** number.

- For the complex number $z = a + ib$, $a = Re(z)$ is the **real** part of z and $b = Im(z)$ is the **imaginary** part of z.

- Real numbers are complex numbers where the imaginary part $b = 0$.

- The **conjugate** of $z = a + ib$, denoted by z^* or $\bar{z}$ is the complex number $\bar{z} = a - ib$.

- z and $\bar{z}$ are called **complex conjugates** or **conjugate pair**.

↝ When a complex number is multiplied with its conjugate, the result is a real number.

Equality of Complex Numbers

Two complex numbers are equal when their **real parts** are equal, and their **imaginary parts** are also equal.

$$a + ib = c + id \text{ if and only if } a = c \text{ and } b = d$$

↝ Inequalities between complex numbers do not exist.

- A complex number is only zero if both the real and imaginary parts are zero

$$\alpha + ib = 0 \text{ if and only if } a = 0 \text{ and } b = 0$$

Operations with complex numbers

Addition: $(\alpha + ib) + (c + id) = (\alpha + c) + i(b + d)$

Subtraction: $(\alpha + bi) - (c + di) = (\alpha - c) + (b - d)i$

Multiplication: $(\alpha + bi)(c + di) = (\alpha c - bd) + (\alpha d + bc)i$

Division: To divide complex numbers, we multiply both the denominator and numerator by the conjugate of the denominator

$$\frac{(\alpha + bi)}{(c + di)} = \frac{(\alpha + bi)(c - di)}{(c + di)(c - di)} = \frac{\alpha c - \alpha di + bci - bdi^2}{c^2 - (di)^2} = \frac{\alpha c + bd}{c^2 + d^2} + \frac{bc - \alpha d}{c^2 + d^2}i$$

Powers of i

$$i^n = i^{4q+r} = i^{4q} \cdot i^r = (i^4)^q \cdot i^r = 1 \cdot i^r = i^r = \begin{cases} 1, & r = 0 \\ i, & r = 1 \\ -1, & r = 2 \\ -i, & r = 3 \end{cases}$$

Properties of Conjugates

Let $z = \alpha + bi$ and $\bar{z} = \alpha - bi$ a conjugate pair and $z_1, z_2 \in \mathbb{C}$:

$z + \bar{z} = 2\alpha$	$z - \bar{z} = 2bi$
$z\bar{z} = \alpha^2 + b^2$	$\overline{z_1 + z_2} = \bar{z}_1 + \bar{z}_2$
$\overline{z_1 - z_2} = \bar{z}_1 - \bar{z}_2$	$\overline{z_1 \cdot z_2} = \bar{z}_1 \cdot \bar{z}_2$
$\overline{\left(\dfrac{z_1}{z_2}\right)} = \dfrac{\bar{z}_1}{\bar{z}_2}$	

The quadratic equation $\alpha z^2 + bz + c = 0$, where $\alpha, b, c \in \mathbb{R}, \alpha \neq 0$ and $z \in \mathbb{C}$

The nature of the roots of the above quadratic equation depends on the value of the expression $b^2 - 4\alpha c$. This expression is called the **discriminant** and is represented by the Greek letter delta Δ.

- If $\Delta > 0$ there are two distinct real roots $z_{1,2} = \dfrac{-b \pm \sqrt{\Delta}}{2\alpha}$

- If $\Delta = 0$ there are two identical real roots $z = \dfrac{-b}{2\alpha}$

- If $\Delta < 0$ there are two complex roots which are conjugates $z_{1,2} = \dfrac{-b \pm i\sqrt{-\Delta}}{2\alpha}$

Complex Conjugate Root Theorem states that if $P(x)$ is a polynomial with real coefficients, and $a + bi$ is a root of $P(x)$ with a and b real numbers, then its complex conjugate $a - bi$ is also a root of $P(x)$.

The Fundamental Theorem of Algebra states that any complex polynomial of degree n has exactly n roots.

Geometrical representation of Complex Numbers ([1]Argand Diagram)

Any Complex number $z = x + yi$ may be represented on the Complex plane, either by using the point $M(x, y)$, or the position vector $\overrightarrow{OM}$. The coordinates of the point $M(x, y)$ are the real $Re(z)$ and the imaginary $Im(z)$ parts of the corresponding complex number.

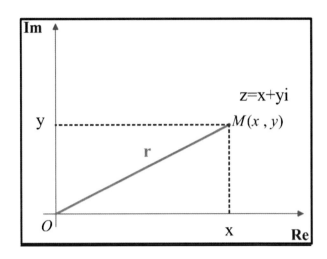

Note: Since complex numbers can be represented as vectors on an Argand diagram, the addition and subtraction of complex numbers may follow the parallelogram law for vectors.

[1]Jean-Robert Argand (1768–1822)

Forms of complex numbers

Cartesian form   {René Descartes (1596-1650)}

The representation of a complex number in Cartesian form is $z = x + yi$

Polar form (Modulus-Argument form)

The **modulus$|z|$** (or magnitude) of complex z is defined as the length of the line segment OM

$$|z| = \left|\overrightarrow{OM}\right| = r = \sqrt{x^2 + y^2}$$

The **argument arg(z)** of complex z is defined as the angle θ that the line segment OM forms with the positive x-axis.

So, the modulus-argument form for a complex number $z = x + yi$ is

$$z = r(\cos\theta + i\sin\theta) = rcis(\theta) \text{ where } -\pi < \theta \leq \pi.$$

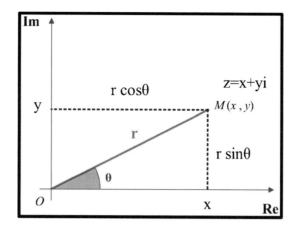

▨ To convert from the **Cartesian** form to the **Polar** form

$$r = \sqrt{x^2 + y^2}, \quad \theta = \arctan\left(\frac{y}{x}\right)$$

▨ To convert from the **Polar** form to the **Cartesian** form

$$x = r\cos\theta$$

$$y = r\sin\theta$$

Exponential form (Euler's)

The exponential form for a complex number **z** with **modulus r** and **argument θ** is

$$z = re^{i\theta}$$

Properties of Modulus and Argument

▨ If $z_1 = r_1(\cos\theta_1 + i\sin\theta_1)$ and $z_2 = r_2(\cos\theta_2 + i\sin\theta_2)$

then

$$z_1 \cdot z_2 = r_1 \cdot r_2(\cos(\theta_1 + \theta_2) + i\sin(\theta_1 + \theta_2))$$

$$\frac{z_1}{z_2} = \frac{r_1}{r_2}(\cos(\theta_1 - \theta_2) + i\sin(\theta_1 - \theta_2))$$

$\|z\| = \|\bar{z}\| = \|-z\|$	$\|z\|^2 = z\bar{z}$	$\|z_1 \cdot z_2\| = \|z_1\| \cdot \|z_2\|$
$\left\|\dfrac{z_1}{z_2}\right\| = \dfrac{\|z_1\|}{\|z_2\|}$	$\|\|z_1\| - \|z_2\|\| \leq \|z_1+z_2\| \leq \|z_1\| + \|z_2\|$	$\arg(z_1 z_2) = \arg(z_1) + \arg(z_2)$
$\arg(z_1{}^n) = n \cdot \arg(z_1)$	$\arg\left(\dfrac{z_1}{z_2}\right) = \arg(z_1) - \arg(z_2)$	$\arg(\bar{z}) = -\arg(z)$
$\arg(z_1 z_2 \cdots z_n) = \arg(z_1) + \arg(z_2) + \cdots + \arg(z_n)$		

De Moivre's Theorem {Abraham de Moivre Leibniz (1667-1754)}

If $z = r(cos\theta + isin\theta)$ then

$$z^n = r^n(cos\theta + isin\theta)^n = r^n(cos\,(n\theta) + isin\,(n\theta))$$

Note: The principle of mathematical induction is used to prove De Moivre's Theorem for $n \in \mathbb{Z}^+$.

When $\|z\| = 1$ we can easily prove the following identities:

$$z + \frac{1}{z} = 2cos\theta$$

$$z - \frac{1}{z} = 2i\,sin\theta$$

$$z^n + \frac{1}{z^n} = 2\cos\,n\,\theta$$

$$z^n - \frac{1}{z^n} = 2i\sin\,n\,\theta$$

Important: The multiplication of a complex number z by another complex number $w = r(cos\theta + isin\theta)$ scales the complex number z by r and rotates z counterclockwise by angle θ.

For example, multiplication by i gives a $90°$ counterclockwise rotation about the origin and similarly, multiplication by $-i$ gives a $90°$ clockwise rotation about the origin.

Roots of unity

Given that $z^n = 1$ then the nth roots of unity are given by the following formula:

$$z = \left(\cos\left(\frac{2k\pi}{n}\right) + isin\left(\frac{2k\pi}{n}\right)\right) \text{ where } k = 0,1,2,\dots,n-1$$

$$\text{or } k = \dots, -2, -1, 0, 1, 2, \dots$$

Note: The nth roots of unity are $\{1,\ e^{\frac{2\pi i}{n}},\ e^{\frac{4\pi i}{n}},\dots,\ e^{\frac{2(n-1)\pi i}{n}}\}$. They are distributed evenly at every $\frac{2\pi}{n}$ radians around the unit circle and form the vertices of a regular $n-$gon.

Roots of a complex number w

Given that $z^n = w = r(cos\theta + isin\theta)$ then the nth roots of complex w are given by the following formula:

$$z = r^{\frac{1}{n}}\left(\cos(\frac{\theta+2k\pi}{n}) + isin(\frac{\theta+2k\pi}{n})\right) \text{ where } k = 0,1,2,\dots,n-1$$

$$\text{or } k = \dots, -2-1, 0, 1, 2, \dots$$

Find the fifth roots of unity and represent them on an Argand diagram.

$z^5 = 1 \Rightarrow$

$$z = \cos\left(\frac{2k\pi}{5}\right) + isin\left(\frac{2k\pi}{5}\right) = \operatorname{cis}\left(\frac{2k\pi}{5}\right) = e^{\frac{2k\pi i}{5}}, k = 0, 1, .., 4 \text{ or } k = -2, -1, 0, 1, 2$$

$$z_0 = \cos(0) + isin(0) = \operatorname{cis}(0) = e^0 = 1$$

$$z_1 = \cos\left(\frac{2\pi}{5}\right) + isin\left(\frac{2\pi}{5}\right) = \operatorname{cis}\left(\frac{2\pi}{5}\right) = e^{\frac{2\pi i}{5}}$$

$$z_2 = \cos\left(\frac{4\pi}{5}\right) + i\sin\left(\frac{4\pi}{5}\right) = \text{cis}\left(\frac{4\pi}{5}\right) = e^{\frac{4\pi i}{5}}$$

$$z_3 = \cos\left(\frac{6\pi}{5}\right) + i\sin\left(\frac{6\pi}{5}\right) = \text{cis}\left(\frac{6\pi}{5}\right) = e^{\frac{6\pi i}{5}}$$

$$z_4 = \cos\left(\frac{8\pi}{5}\right) + i\sin\left(\frac{8\pi}{5}\right) = \text{cis}\left(\frac{8\pi}{5}\right) = e^{\frac{8\pi i}{5}}$$

The fifth roots of unity are represented in the following Argand diagram:

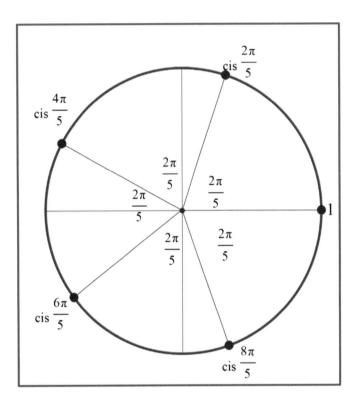

References

1. Mathematics HL formula booklet, First examinations 2014, Diploma Programme, International Baccalaureate®.

2. Mathematics HL guide, First examinations 2014, Diploma Programme, International Baccalaureate®.

3. TI-84 Plus and TI-84 Plus Silver Edition Guidebook.

Made in the USA
Monee, IL
02 December 2019